I0445554

GREGG WESTWOOD

ROOTED
SOUL

Weaving Sacred Threads and
Conscious Embodiment into Oneness

Copyright © 2025 by Gregg Westwood.

All rights reserved. No part of this book may be reproduced or used in any manner without written permission of the copyright owner except for the use of quotations in a book review. For more information, contact: gregg@depthintegration.com.

ISBN Paperback: 979-8-9930995-0-7
ISBN Electronic: 979-8-9930995-1-4

Library of Congress Control Number: 2025919830

Publishing Consultant: PRESStinely, PRESStinely.com

Portions of this book are works of nonfiction. Certain names and identifying characteristics have been changed.

Printed in the United States of America.

Gregg Westwood MA
Embodied Soul Integration
DepthIntegration.com

Depth
Integration

Contents

FOREWORD

By DaeEss 1Dréa Pennington Wasio, MD

When a man chooses to dive beneath the noise of the world, beneath the expectations, distractions, and patterns he inherited, that's not just healing. That's revolutionary.

Gregg's journey in *Rooted Soul* is exactly that: a deeply personal, vulnerable, and courageous act of reclamation. In these pages, you won't find dogma or prescriptions. What you will find is the lived experience of a man who dared to pause, look within, and unravel the knots of pain, projection, and programming in order to reclaim his authentic essence.

When Gregg and I first connected, I saw in him what I see in so many who come to this work: a longing. A desire to serve. To find peace. To make sense of life. To move beyond survival into something soul-rooted and meaningful. Over the years, I witnessed his courage in confronting the shadows, telling the truth, and softening into something deeper than performance—presence.

Reading *Rooted Soul* feels like sitting beside a fire that warms and challenges you all at once; it invites you to remember what's essential and to reclaim the parts of yourself you may have forgotten along the way.

This book is both a memoir and a medicine offering. Through stories, insights, and reflections, Gregg walks us through the rites of passage that many of us face but few dare to name: grief, addiction, disconnection, identity collapse, spiritual awakening. And yet, through it all, there's an undercurrent of grace.

The way Gregg writes, you feel like you're sitting across from him, heart to heart. No mask. No performance. Just truth. And in that truth, we remember our own.

If you're holding this book, it's likely because your soul, too, is asking for deeper roots. A clearer voice. A softer heart. And a braver path forward.

So take a breath. Let these pages speak to the part of you that already knows. Let them remind you that your soul, too, has roots: ancient, resilient, and endlessly alive.

With reverence for your healing journey,

Dr. DaeEss 1Dréa
Integrative Physician, Author, and Sacred Medicine Retreat Leader
www.1Drea.com

This book is dedicated to Source, the Creator, Great Spirit.

INTRODUCTION

Ever since I can remember, I have wanted to live from a place of love and compassion and to help others do the same.

In this book, I share how my sacred journey of immersing myself in ancient spiritual and modern psychological traditions has assisted me in expanding past the preconceptions I had of myself and the Universe.

The words I share come from my personal experience combined with decades of education and training. I emphasize the significance of remaining connected to my body, the Earth, and all her living beings while heeding their wisdom. I share the benefits of embracing and receiving guidance from the spiritual realm, along with the beings and energies that are present.

This book doesn't offer a quick-fix solution for the challenges of the human experience. Instead, it recognizes and acknowledges that the spiritual journey is continuously evolving and ever-expanding; a lifelong path that may unfold across many lifetimes of exploration.

I intend to pose questions and stretch your perception of what reality is, as many of us adhere to societal rules, suffer from ancestral wounds, and hold beliefs that are not grounded in the Divine.

My hope is this book inspires you in expanding your sense of self and gives you new ideas of how to live more authentically and interact with this planet and all of its living beings with the utmost respect.

> *"The present moment is filled with joy and happiness.*
> *If you are present, you will see it."*
> —Thich Nhat Hanh

The Wound

Leaving My Body

As I had many times before, I lay on the treatment table, closed my eyes, and took a deep breath. The room was dim. A gentle candle flame flickered from a table close to my feet. Doc Kim placed her hand gently on my abdomen just above my sacrum. I trembled as a tingling wave of fear overtook me. I gasped, struggling to breathe. Heavy, suffocating energy closed in on me, pushing my body into the table.

I was transported to the early 1960s. I saw and felt a large hairy arm brushing forcefully over my mouth. I knew: *This is terribly wrong.* I wanted to scream. There was no one to hear me. I wanted to reach out, but no one was there to save me. Without words or understanding, I left my body.

An electric current shot through me, returning me to the present moment. I sprang up and gasped, "Doctor." The sensory memory of my pediatrician doing something very inappropriate flooded my mind and body. Instantly, my body knew. I had been abused.

In numerous instances of abuse, children disconnect from their bodies because they don't have the capacity to tolerate their sensations. In order to survive, pieces of them fragment. But the pain remains in their bodies. I, like many others, struggled to be present after this trauma.

Pre-verbal wounds have less concrete memory, and thus are challenging to remember. *Was it a dream?* My thirty-year-old mind was reluctant to accept this childhood sense memory, but the chronic pain in my sacrum had served as the gateway to bring my awareness to the source of my wound.

When I informed Mom about this the next day, she said, "You know, he left town quickly one day." The truth of my non-verbal memory was confirmed—my body had not lied. My innocence had been stolen. And, as I hadn't healed from this abuse as a toddler, future experiences compounded the wound—as a child, I believed the world was not safe.

At this young age I sensed Mom was very fearful, as well. Mom loved expressiveness. She worried when I wasn't "on." So I learned that if I shared my vulnerability, I wouldn't receive her love. Again, it was before I had words. The tenets of pre- and perinatal psychology[1] propose that we sense and often absorb the feeling states of our mothers. I found out later why.

Despite her fears, Mom loved being a mother more than anything. Nothing gave her more joy. My brother arrived when I was three and my sister when I was four and a half years old. The three of us grew up in a house of deep love. My parents met in kindergarten, and their love for each other was obvious. Dad worshiped the ground Mom walked on, and they frequently told us, "We love you more than you will ever know."

Being the oldest child came with responsibility. That responsibility was accompanied by stress.

---

[1] *Prenatal and Perinatal Psychology:* The study of psychological development and experiences during the prenatal and perinatal periods, focusing on how these early stages impact later emotional and psychological health.

Shame and Humiliation

It was a bright, sunny day, as the little girls and boys of my kindergarten class gathered in a circle for a milk and cookies break. As I opened my milk carton, I noticed my teacher hovering over me. Something was terribly wrong. As I lifted my gaze, I saw her disapproving glare, her left hand on her hip, and her right finger pointing at a puddle on the floor in front of me. She called out," What is that, Gregg?"

I had wet my pants.

Humiliated, I froze. Every muscle became stiff as waves of warmth flushed up from my toes to my face. My shoulders rose to my ears as I gasped for air and stopped breathing. My heart pounded, and all my body's systems began shutting down. My jaw clenched, my lips pursed, my eyes crossed inside my head, and my mind went blank. I could sense everyone staring at me. Their silence was deafening. I searched frantically for what seemed like hours for the right words that would not expose me for what had just happened.

As my head dropped in shame, I saw my milk carton. "I spilled my milk," I said, staring at the floor. She retorted, "That is not milk!" and gestured for me to leave the circle. Of course, the puddle was not milk; it wasn't white. I shut my eyes, trying to become invisible, as my teacher pulled me by the arm to the bathroom to change my wet pants.

Then, during the car ride home, the girls in my carpool giggled and pointed, telling the mother driving, "Gregg had to change his clothes!" Their laughter felt like sharp needles, embedding shame into every part of my being.

My innocence had been stolen, and this traumatic memory lived in my body for almost sixty years.

The wound affected my nervous system. Anxiety caused me to lose control of my bladder. I became a chronic bedwetter. Each time I woke up Mom to tell her I wet the bed, my humiliation and shame deepened.

Shame heightened my sensitivity to potential dangers in my surroundings and the emotional reactions of those around me. For example, when my parents traveled, they often left me with Mom's parents overnight. Grandma Tommie and Grandpa Harland consumed a significant amount of alcohol. While everything appeared to be fine during the day, their nighttime drinking often spiraled into chaos.

One such evening, as we sat on the couch watching *Hee Haw*,[2] their laughter shifted to an eerie tenor. Suddenly, my grandparents began chasing me and smacking me with flyswatters. It wasn't funny anymore. Dashing to escape my big grandpa, I ducked under the dining room table to avoid being hit. I covered my head and curled up in a ball, waiting for what seemed like hours for him to stop.

After returning from World War II, Grandpa Harland drank a bottle of vodka each night. In his drunken stupors he shouted belligerently, slurring his favorite phrase "in laws, outlaws, chickenshits, and nincompoops." One night, he even went out to the backyard and shot his rifle. Grandpa's drunken outbursts instilled panic in me.

My panic deepened the following Christmas morning. While opening our presents, Grandpa staggered over to the Christmas tree and began pulling it down haphazardly. Attempting to protect us, Dad yelled at my drunk grandpa to stop. Seething, Dad's face flushed red, and his neck veins bulged.

His anger only fueled Grandpa's stupor. Dad grabbed Grandpa's arm, and they struggled. They were yelling back and forth, and it scared me. I

---

[2] *Hee-Haw* was an American television variety show that aired from 1969 to 1992, blending country music and comedy, featuring sketches and performances centered on rural life.

wanted it to stop. *How do I make it stop?* Eventually, everyone froze, not knowing what to do or say.

I began absorbing their feelings for them, shouldering their burdens, hoping I could calm them. I took my brother and sister into the kitchen to get them away from the tree and the yelling and brought them a toy to play with. Mom was in the kitchen, preparing the Christmas breakfast, and I could see her trembling, so I put my hand on her back until she stopped. I absorbed her upset. This pattern evolved into a caretaker relationship dynamic: if I provided emotional support, I would be safeguarded and provided for in return. I knew how to take care of others, but my shame made me neglect my feelings.

Dimming My Light

Looking back, despite my shame, I was an effervescent boy with a vivid imagination. I loved dancing, acting, and singing so much. When I was six, my dad taught me a song—the lyrics were our address, in case I ever got lost. I still remember every note.

I loved imitating characters I watched on television, pretending I was in their world. In grade school, I learned about other countries and their traditions. My parents' best friends lived in Tahiti, and I imagined living there as I danced the hula. One day at show and tell, I shared the tikis, photos, and shell leis they sent us, taught my third-grade classmates the hula, and told them about my weekend trip to Tahiti. Of course, a weekend trip to Tahiti didn't happen in the "real" world. Looking back, I'm so grateful that my teacher, Mrs. White, just smiled. No humiliation in front of my classmates this time.

Girls were the only kids my age in our neighborhood, so I grew up playing jacks and dress up. One of my parents' friends said to them, "You know Gregg's gay..." Upset at the comment, my parents denied it, and Dad began trying to teach me how to kick the football. It was his way of molding me into a boy. I was terrible, missing the ball almost every time.

However, I did like the cheerleaders. They looked like they were having fun with their pom poms, jumping and kicking, and their yells—"Let's go, Tigers!"

In the 1960s and 70s, our family went to church every Sunday, and after the service, the whole family gathered for a meal. While the women cooked, the men watched NFL football. Gathered around the black-and-white console television, the men cheered the Kansas City Chiefs and yelled at the referees. I gathered towels, transformed them into pom poms, and played cheerleader. The exuberance of my soul radiated through joyous leaps, high kicks, and vibrant dancing. I was alive and filled with joy. Delighting in the rush of excitement pulsing through my body, I extended my energy beyond my limbs, hands, fingers, feet, and toes.

One Sunday, stopping to catch my breath after a particularly exuberant cheerleading dance, I sensed the disapproval of Grandpa Joe, Dad's father. As I made eye contact, he glared back. I stopped dancing and fled to the kitchen. I knew at that moment I didn't fit—I was inherently wrong. I know now that the little cheerleader in me had been expressing his feminine side, and for Grandpa Joe and Grandpa Harland, that was unacceptable. From then on, I rendered myself invisible in their presence.

Spending my time in the kitchen with Mom, my grandmothers, and aunts provided me with a sense of acceptance. These remarkable women offered me support in ways the men in my life did not. As Grandma Tommie prepared her famous fried chicken, we discussed the arts, shared thoughts on the latest fashions, expressed our feelings, and indulged in a bit of gossip. It felt like home. Grandma Tommie taught me about dedication, service, and joy. As a head nurse, she took impeccable care of people everyday. She instilled joy in taking me to the zoo and shopping for clothes—I loved trying on new clothes!

My grandmothers and the women in my life were a support system for me, and they, along with Dad, helped me nurture my creativity. My paternal grandmother, Kate, for example, was an accomplished cellist, actress, acting teacher, singer, and choral director. Her father had been a talented painter. My dad was a creative genius, truly from another planet. I still am in awe of his ability to draw and paint anything from scratch, to make everyone laugh hysterically at his jokes, and to excel in all of this with such graceful ease. My creativity, talents, and abilities were born out of and passed down from this amazing lineage of artists, but especially from Dad.

Putdowns Led to Self-Doubt

Dad and I were deeply close, our relationship filled with love and respect. He was a drummer. As a teenager, I played the French horn in the school band. We were both actors. He taught me about life through our shared love for the arts, creativity, imagination, psychology, and the cosmos. But whenever I felt too much joy or displayed too much confidence, he'd flip into someone else and put me in my place, saying, "Who do you think you are, *'Big Time'*?" His putdown hit me like a hammer in the back. In our family, there were "correct ways" of doing things. My father was the arbiter of where the boundaries were, and he had a short fuse.

For example, I recall being told one autumn day to rake leaves. Suddenly, Dad was in front of me, reprimanding me for doing it the "wrong way." These sudden outbursts startled me, leaving me paralyzed in fear. I tiptoed on eggshells, acutely aware of the potential danger waiting in the shadows. His sudden putdowns chipped away at my joy, reinforcing my belief that I was flawed. I began to tread carefully, doubting myself at every turn.

I couldn't trust my instincts. I shut down. Throughout my life, challenging experiences compounded this initial wound. Concealing my shame, I withdrew into an empty, protective shell. I often spent significant time in my room, isolating from a world that felt threatening. My mother worried about me—she worried about everything. Her worrying manifested in asking me several times if I did one thing—"Did you remember to..."—followed by constant check-ins: "Are you sure you..."

It was as though she didn't trust me to do something correctly, which deepened my lack of trust in myself.

The week I turned eight, we moved to a bigger home. This beautiful house, built in the 1920s, was two stories with four bedrooms, one of which became my first private space. The house's white stucco was highlighted by a black roof and window shutters with a red brick staircase leading to the red front door. Across the street lay a spacious private park, featuring a small creek meandering through its center. An arched wooden bridge linked the homes on the opposite side. The park was adorned with numerous maple, elm, oak, and weeping willow trees. It was every kid's dream playland.

The following week I began the third grade and found out this neighborhood had only boys my age. When they played football in the park, I still played cheerleader—I wasn't a fan of tackling. They laughed at me. I didn't know how to play with boys, and with their teasing my feelings of shame intensified into an uncomfortable fear of being seen and judged.

Eating became my way of silencing the fear inside me. I saw my father eating continually, so I followed his example. He hid his snacks, so I hid my eating. After school, I would grab cookies and candy and shelter in my room. My Uncle Jack used to greet me with the remark, "You just keep getting fatter." I earned the nickname "Roly Poly" from those boys in my neighborhood, and the teasing about my weight deepened my wounds.

My body was a target of shame, making the thought of being around others frightening. So, I isolated myself further. Uninterested in playing with the other kids my age, I hung out with my parents and their friends. I missed out on a lot of childhood. I don't remember much about the next few years besides being in my room with my French horn and cookies and occasionally performing in a play.

Hiding Who I Truly Was

In seventh grade, the annual play was a trilogy of Dr. Seuss stories. I was cast as the captain in *Bartholomew and the Oobleck*.[3] The director, a talented ninth-grade girl, asked if I would mind playing the captain effeminately. I said, "Sure, why not?" I enjoyed the challenge. I embodied the effeminate captain with an exaggerated lisp and flowing gestures with a flick from the tips of my fingers. I was delighted to experience this jovial character. I went full out, no holding back. *Why should I?* I was an actor and had to play the part with my entire being. It is what great actors did. And I was going to be a great actor. The worlds I created were so much safer than the world I lived in. I found safety in being someone else. In my imagination, I explored these magical realms and became comfortable expressing my creative, sensitive, and feminine sides.

After my performance, I was heading down a hallway when three big, ninth-grade football players wearing royal blue letter jackets sneered as they passed me. "Is that a boy or a girl?" I know now that was the moment that I chose to be seen as a boy. I shut down my feminine side and created a mask that hid who I truly was inside. I would wear it for much of my life.

The Secret

At this vulnerable age of fourteen, my developing sexuality became attached to my growing series of childhood wounds. One afternoon after junior high school, my friend Clifford and I snuck into my parents' room,

---

[3] *Bartholomew and the Oobleck* is a children's book by Dr. Seuss that tells the story of a young boy named Bartholomew who deals with a sticky, green substance called Oobleck that falls from the sky, causing chaos in his kingdom.

searching for treasure. In my Dad's closet, we found a joint in one of his shoes and, hidden in the corner by a heavy winter coat, several *Penthouse* and *Playboy* magazines. *Why is Dad hiding these in his closet? It must not be safe for others to know that he looks at them. And if he's hiding this, it must be wrong...*

As Clifford became excited looking at the photos of the naked women, I realized I didn't have those feelings. In one of the *Playboys* there was an insert for the new magazine *Playgirl*. I had a feeling for those men. This feeling felt familiar to the feelings I felt for a character in my favorite cartoon *Jonny Quest*,[4] Race Bannon. Race was a special agent assigned to safeguard Dr. Quest, a famous scientist, Jonny, and his friend Haji on their extraordinary adventures around the world. I was attracted to his deep voice, muscular physique, and how he risked his life to protect Jonny. I was beginning to put the pieces together in my adolescent mind but knew this biological urge I was feeling was something I should hide.

Little did I know that these secrets would attach to my wound. When I was already questioning who I was, the discovery of my father's magazines added another layer of confusion and shame. My attraction to male bodies in magazines would later turn into a habit, tying my burgeoning identity to secrecy and fear.

Growing up gay in the 60s and 70s was a secretive and shameful experience. There was barely any mention of our existence—there were only putdowns like "faggot" for being too effeminate. I began fantasizing about big, strong men taking care of me and found images of muscular men, some naked, soothing me when I felt overwhelmed or helpless. I know now that I was reaching out, hoping to absorb their pseudo-strength into the holes my fragmentation created. Of course, once the pseudo-soothing wore off, my insecurities were enhanced. I was gay, alone, and scared.

---

[4] *Johnny Quest* was an animated adventure television series created by Hanna-Barbera in the 1960s, focusing on the adventures of a young boy and his team as they explore exotic locations and confront villains.

My secret amplified my fear of being seen. My lower back contracted, and I developed a knot of anxiety in my stomach and chest. Not having the capacity to feel, I neglected my wellbeing, and I started smoking. But the smoke only deepened the ache in my chest. What I wanted was to breathe deeply and freely—a longing I didn't yet understand. I discovered solace in the theater, immersing myself in the various characters I brought to life. On stage, I came alive. I became bigger than my body.

I learned to amplify my voice to speak or sing to the back of the house. The applause from the audience and praise for my talent gave me the love and nurturance I craved from the world. I found solace and safety in being someone else onstage adorned in make up. My imagination became my sanctuary—a space where I could rewrite my story and escape the confines of my shame, if only briefly.

However, even after playing Freddy in *My Fair Lady*[5] and landing the lead role of Albert Peterson, in my high school's production of *Bye Bye Birdie*,[6] I couldn't escape the voice that whispered, "It's not enough."

Looking back, I see how all these early wounds shaped my path. The theater gave me a stage to explore who I was even as I hid from myself, but the journey to reclaim wholeness was just beginning.

"Children don't get traumatized because they are hurt.
They get traumatized because they're alone with the hurt."
—Dr. Gabor Mate

[5] *My Fair Lady* is a musical adaptation of George Bernard Shaw's play *Pygmalion*, with music by Frederick Loewe and lyrics by Alan Jay Lerner, telling the story of a phonetics professor who transforms a flower girl into a refined lady.
[6] *Bye Bye Birdie* is a musical comedy created by Michael Stewart, featuring music by Charles Strouse and lyrics by Lee Adams, revolving around the fictional rock star Conrad Birdie and his fans during the 1950s.

2

Returning to My Body

After graduating from high school, I spent a year at our family's church college, at Grandma Kate's request. She was the RLDS world church's[7] women's director—the most powerful woman in the church. I was her only grandchild who attended Graceland—a small college in a very small town in Iowa. My parents went there and were icons. Everyone knew them, and everyone at Graceland saw me through them. I felt like my parents' child there more than myself.

I did perform in *Li'l Abner*[8] and marched in the band at Graceland but felt out of place and longed to find my own identity. After one year in Iowa, I moved back to my home town, Columbia, and enrolled in the University of Missouri. Jumping from a small college to a major university was a challenging adjustment, especially since I didn't have a major. The classes were huge and impersonal. I joined a fraternity, and my straight As turned to Cs. Fortunately, a director from high school asked me to play the role of Matt in the local theater company's production of *The Fantasticks*.[9]

[7] The *Reorganized Church of Jesus Christ of Latter Day Saints*, now known as Community of Christ, is a Christian denomination that emerged from the Latter Day Saint movement in the 19th century, emphasizing peace, justice, and community service.
[8] *Li'l Abner* was a comic strip created by Al Capp featuring the humorous lives of residents in the fictional Appalachian town of Dogpatch, which ran from 1934 to 1977 and was adapted into a musical and film.
[9] *The Fantasticks* was a musical created by Tom Jones and Harvey Schmidt, which debuted in 1960, known for its simple plot about two young lovers and their over-protective parents, featuring iconic songs like "Try to Remember."

Dance

In the audience of our closing-night performance sat my soon-to-be-dance teachers. Kay Henderson and Michael Simms saw potential in me and after the performance they came backstage and offered me a full three-year dance scholarship at Stephens College. I was struck and elated. *Finally*. This is what I wanted most in life. Stephens College, a famous women's college in Columbia, Missouri, had a rich tradition in theater and dance.

As preparation for my scholarship the next fall, I was required to take classes the preceding spring. I started my weight-loss journey to achieve a "dancer's body," as I had a few pounds to shed. At nineteen, I was seen as old to begin dancing, especially since most of the girls had started their training at the age of three. As I entered my first ballet class, I felt intimidated and self-conscious. Tights, a dance belt, and leg warmers was not my typical attire, but it would become my wardrobe for the next several years.

I felt pride when Michael asked me to demonstrate "turn out" for the class. I pretended to purposely place my heels together, but I am naturally turned out at the hips. The girls envied me for having something they spent their entire lives trying to achieve. My duck walk that my pediatricians had attempted to cure with corrective shoes was coming in handy.

Across the ballet studio I spotted the only other guy in class, a thin, handsome man with shoulder-length blond hair. Sensuality emanated from his pores. He was known as KC.

After class, he approached me carrying a GI Joe lunch box like a purse. My eyes were drawn to the chain that encircled his crotch. His eyes twinkled mischievously as he winked and greeted me with "Heeyyy..." I had never been "hit on" by a man before, and he knew it.

KC invited me back to his room at the boys dorm, in a house on campus. As he opened his door, time slowed down and began to pulsate. I had entered a new dimension. A spinning disco ball, hanging from the middle of the ceiling, sprayed rays of light on his drawings of space creatures and punk rock posters that adorned the pink walls. GI Joes were placed strategically, and lava candles created an eerie yet surreal atmosphere. KC offered me a joint to relax. He proceeded to blare music this Midwestern boy had never heard. DEVO, Grace Jones, Prince, and David Bowie; all were quite avant-garde for the early 80s. I didn't grasp their lyrics, but I was intrigued.

Who is this guy, and where is he from? I thought. KC was definitely from another planet. His creativity was otherworldly, and his sensual freedom was intimating at first. I felt cautious and excited at the same time.

Over the next two years, our relationship blossomed, and we became great friends. We were opposites; he opened my eyes to new dimensions, and I brought him down to earth.

I became acquainted with his wounds. KC had been a prostitute and lived off of wealthy gay men until they found another "boy toy" to replace him. Underneath his sexual prowess was a little boy trying to survive in a world he didn't fit into. I related to his out-of-place feeling, and we were spit on more than once by college boys for being faggots. *Why is he attracted to me, this husky boy?* I would wonder.

Still overweight with a couple of months off before our summer session, the ballet master, Michael Simms, took me under his wing in a sort of summer bootcamp. He loved me while using criticism to motivate me, and he began to turn me into a ballet dancer. I had class with him daily, sweated in the sauna, and lost 15 more pounds. I was down to 130 pounds, but still thought I was fat.

Perry Mansfield

After my ballet bootcamp, KC and I rode the bus together to Steamboat Springs, Colorado, for our summer school. Perry Mansfield was founded in the 1940s, and many famous dancers from the Humphrey Weidman modern dance lineage, like Jose Limon, came every summer to perform in the crisp mountain air. Famous actors, like Robert Redford, sent their young daughters to ride horses and take acting and dancing lessons. I was cast as the lead, Captain "Big Jim" Warrington, in the musical *Little Mary Sunshine*[10] alongside Polly Segal, George Segal's daughter.

Perry Mansfield is where I fell in love with Colorado. The brilliant blue skies, warm days and cool nights, snow-capped mountains, gurgling streams, and waterfalls touched my senses and my soul in ways Missouri didn't. Classes all day, rehearsals all night—being in the mountains made it so tolerable.

However, the dry mountain air cracked the girls' toes and their ballet shoes stained with blood. A dancer's life is grueling—not for the faint of heart. But the magic we created was worth the pain. All of the sacrifice led to our main performance for the community.

The ensemble amplified the magic of the performance. What I loved most about dancing was moving together. Having a solo is wonderful, but sensing each others' arms and legs as we danced as one, that lit me up. Aligning precisely, stretching the limits of the human body, and touching the audience—that made my heart sing. We were a family. That bond from performing together is still active today.

After the performance, we had our one day off for the summer. We all rented a hotel room on Steamboat Mountain. KC made friends with anyone, especially if they had drugs. When we arrived, he handed us all little cards that read, "Have a nice trip!" and inside was a present. This was my first "trip" with mushrooms. While the others partied, I was entranced by what I was observing in my friends. I saw their emotions magnified. For me, mushrooms weren't a drug. They heightened my senses and my consciousness.

---

[10] *Little Mary Sunshine* was a musical comedy created by Jim Lunsford and produced in the 1960s, which satirizes the melodramatic conventions of early 20th-century musicals and tells the story of a young girl in a small town facing various challenges.

When I returned home to Columbia, I was exhausted. The summer in Steamboat was packed with new and exciting experiences. After two weeks off to recover, I began my scholarship and moved into a house with the other male dancers, affectionately known as the "Voo Voo house." Along with KC, there was Chaz, Michael, Romeo, and Keith. Chaz was the emotional, temperamental dancer, Michael the ballet diva, and Keith the tap dancer. Romeo was the most beautiful Filipino girl in drag, and together with his flamboyant "sister" Ricardo, they fooled even the keenest eye.

I was the conservative one.

We partied hard, danced on the dining room tables at the cafeteria to the songs from *Fame*[11] and *Flashdance*.[12] We were cool, and all of the girls wanted to hang out with us. Many of the girls were convinced I wasn't gay. One evening, just before we were headed out to dance, one girl pinned me down on the couch in our basement, shaking me as she shouted, "You're not gay. You're not gay!" If I wasn't gay before...

"By George," the local disco, was our home almost every night. We took over the dance floor perfecting the latest moves, taking up space, intimidating the others, but they were impressed. On the night of my birthday, Ricardo took over the DJ's microphone and proclaimed, "This next song is dedicated to Gregg Westwood. Tonight is his birthday!" The speakers blasted "I'm Coming Out" by Diania Ross. My coming out was not my choice, and it was loud.

Embarrassed, I forced a smile. I waved nervously to everyone who was standing, laughing, and clapping, then scrambled to find the nearest seat to hide. A hand touched my knee. As I slowly raised my head, I saw

---

[11] *Fame*, directed by Alan Parker (Los Angeles: Metro-Goldwyn-Mayer, 1980) is a musical drama film portraying the struggles and ambitions of students at New York's High School of Performing Arts, exploring themes of talent, perseverance, and the costs of pursuing fame.
[12] *Flashdance*, directed by Adrian Lyne (Hollywood: Paramount Pictures, 1983). A romantic drama about a young woman in Pittsburgh who works as a welder by day and a dancer by night, the film became iconic for its music, dance sequences, and theme of chasing dreams against the odds.

a leopard mini dress. The dress accentuated her dark brown skin and her pearly white teeth. Her "heh heh heh" cackle lightened me up, which was her intention. This was Kim, aka Miss Wonderful.

Kim was from a family of African American farmers from the suburbs of St. Louis. I did not know there were African American farmers. Her church sponsored her to attend our affluent school. Each night I didn't have a rehearsal, we hung out in her dorm room and posed questions about the meaning of life. She frequently posed the question "Who are you?" Our friendship was unconditional. I found out what unconditional love was when I left her at a bar one night to go home with a man. The next day, ashamed at my selfishness, I expected her to be angry with me. Instead, she met me with, "Did you have fun? He was hot!" She became my best friend.

Kim loved visiting my parents. My father's jokes had her in stitches. They loved her. My parents had broken the cycle of racism from my lineage.

I will never forget the day I said the "N" word. I was six years old, in the backseat of the family car, laughing with a classmate, waiting for Mom to pick up dry-cleaning at the drive-up window. She suddenly turned, reached across her seat, and slapped me. "Never say that word again!" Mom glared straight into my eyes. I didn't. That was the only time Mom ever slapped me. Every time I hear the word, I cringe, not only for its hateful connotation, but I feel the slap.

Kim also helped me come out to my parents. The day I came out to my parents, my mother gave me a hug. She knew. On the other hand, my father, the sociologist, felt the male dancers were influencing me. Feeling hurt by his discomfort, I withdrew from him. It only took him a couple of days before he reached out in tears saying, "I love you, no matter what. I just don't want you to get hurt."

The Nutcracker

During that senior year at Stephens, I had the incredible opportunity to dance the role of the Snow King in *The Nutcracker*. It was a dream role. During rehearsals, I embraced the role of the *danseur noble*, guiding the Snow Queen, danced by "Big Al"—she was ninety pounds, through her graceful pirouettes and lifting her overhead effortlessly with just one hand. Maintaining the flow of choreography in sync with the music demanded both focus and surrender, leaving me feeling blissful. I was elated because jumping was my specialty. In the air, I felt an exhilarating sense of unbounded freedom. It was as though my heavy physical form dissolved into light as I soared across the stage. We rehearsed each day and night for our upcoming performances in early December.

While practicing the lift for the closing of Act One, Michael stopped me and said, "Face backstage when you lift Allison so we can showcase your best side." He was alluding to my backside. I felt a confusing mix of appreciation and embarrassment; Michael was attracted to me, but I felt shame for being viewed as an object. Was this about my dancing skills or my physical appearance? Little did I realize back then that I would end up doing the same to others—objectifying them.

We took a break from rehearsals for Thanksgiving. During Thanksgiving dinner, I received a call from Michael. The Sugar Plum Prince had broken his leg. "Could you take on that role as well?" I agreed and dove back into an intense rehearsal bootcamp to prepare for the leading male role. Michael assigned me several minor roles throughout the production, so I didn't have time to be nervous.

The Gregg Cracker

My performance was a whirlwind of quick costume changes, brief moments to catch my breath, and rapid shifts in character as I dashed back onstage. I have no idea how I pulled it off, but the show soon earned the affectionate nickname, "The Gregg Cracker." After the opening night performance, my gleaming parents came backstage and told me they were softly shouting, "Fly, Gregg, fly!"

This filled me with great joy, yet I found it difficult to embrace the moment. I had flat feet and low arches, so my legs didn't achieve a perfect ballet line. Before the performance, Michael provided me pads to place on the tops of my feet, giving them the appearance of a point. For me, what should have been a moment of celebration instead had an underlying tone of unworthiness. The mixed messages of love and self-criticism left me doubting my abilities, even as I achieved success. I believed I could never be a great dancer—even though I was. Even when others believed in my talents, I didn't believe in myself. While excelling in most everything I attempted, I never quite felt fulfilled. Still, being on stage and sharing my work with an audience felt like home for me. In each character, I was given the wonderful gift of a safe space to express the many sides of myself I'd had to keep hidden.

Performing on stage, I felt I was in a different dimension from the audience. I relished inviting and coaxing them to join me in my magical reality, time, and space. In performing, I received love. It was not me per se, but my talent to embody a feeling, expand it, and touch people. In performing, there was also the burning question, "Did I do a good job?" If I did, I received applause; if I didn't, they could boo. While I was beginning to inhabit my body, it was still through characters. I chose not to wear my contact lenses, so I couldn't see the audience if they happened to disapprove.

While performing my roles in plays and musicals from a young boy through my high school years had sparked my creativity and imagination, becoming a dancer in college helped me reconnect with my body. This was not a singular event; instead, it was an evolution into an ongoing relationship with my conscious awareness, body, and spirit. I realize now that my interest in non-ordinary states of being began on the stage.

These non-ordinary states fueled my pursuit of a career, despite my fears. After graduation, half of the dancers were moving to New York and half to Los Angeles. Los Angeles dancers performed on television, and their style was primarily jazz. Think back to Solid Gold Dancers. New York dancers performed musical theater on Broadway and with dance companies in concert halls.[13]

I was in the New York group. In order to audition for major musicals, an Actor Equity card was needed. (Actors Equity is the union for actors and dancers.) The summer after graduation, I was cast in my first professional musical *The Unsinkable Molly Brown*[14] in Kansas City at the Waldo Astoria Dinner Playhouse. Since the Waldo was an Actors Equity approved house, I received my card. The stage of the dinner theatre was small, and performing a show every night along with a couple of matinees each week became a job. The confined stage restrained my dancing, and the thrill I once felt began to fade into routine. After each show, I returned to Grandma Kate's house where I lived for the summer. She was so proud of me and attended at least five performances.

A week before my flight to New York, the show's run completed, and I sat in her living room, head in my hands, bawling. "What am I doing, and can I even do this?" I was trembling. Much to my surprise, Grandma came over, sat on the couch next to me, and put her arm around me. She listened to my fears and assured me I would be fine. We hadn't shared this kind of intimacy before. Her wise words and embrace soothed me, and I found the courage to fly to New York City to pursue a professional career in dance and acting.

---

[13] *Solid Gold* (Los Angeles: Paramount Television, 1980–88) was a syndicated American music television program notable for its troupe of "Solid Gold Dancers," who performed choreographed routines to Top 40 hits, blending popular music with flashy, highly stylized dance performances.

[14] *The Unsinkable Molly Brown* was a musical based on the life of Margaret "Molly" Brown, known for her survival of the Titanic disaster and her philanthropic efforts, with music by Meredith Willson.

New York City

The next day, I drove to my parents' to pack my bags. On the day of my flight, my parents gave me $200 and two long hugs. We held each other tight, wiping away the tears. They were happy for me and didn't want to let go.

Chaz picked me up at the airport and drove me to his place in Park Slope, Brooklyn. He graciously offered me a room until I found a job and an apartment. As a young man in my twenties, the thrill of the city was exhilarating, with each block offering a new adventure. I took classes, auditioned for renowned figures like Bob Fosse, performed in small venues, danced with the Deborah Carr modern company, and even played several small roles on the ABC television soap opera *One Life to Live.*[15]

Although I achieved a great deal as a dancer and actor in New York City, looking back, I see that I didn't always commit myself—I'd give up just before reaching a significant breakthrough. I felt that my childhood wounds were preventing me from moving forward—I wasn't good enough; I'd never be good enough. And even though my family supported me emotionally, I still felt the weight of those unhealed familial wounds, like there was a subtle debilitating energy that stopped my progress whenever I gained momentum.

I, like many people who have dealt with childhood trauma, first attempted to heal my wounds with my mind.

---

[15] *One Life to Live* was an American daytime soap opera created by Agnes Nixon that aired from 1968 to 2012 on ABC-TV, known for its diverse characters and storylines that addressed social issues, reflecting the lives and relationships of the residents of the fictional town of Llanview, Pennsylvania.

Most of us try to figure out why we suffer—why we experience pain and repeat patterns that block any true fulfillment in our lives. We attempt to solve them through cognitive understanding, trying to find safety in thinking through our challenges with our rational minds instead of feeling. But we can't think our way toward transformation. The mind can only heal what it can conceive. If we could think our way out of our wounds, they'd be gone. And because many of our challenges have a pre-verbal origin, that's yet another reason the mind alone cannot heal us.

At some point, I realized this. I wanted to heal, so I sought out a spiritual therapist.

Jackie was my first therapist. I told her that as a young boy, I'd wanted to emulate and live my life like Jesus or Martin Luther King, Jr. They were the role models for how to live from my heart, with compassion and love. She said, "Well, that is wonderful, but you'll die young, like they did."

Wow, so being who I want to be will get me killed? Jackie's statement lurked in my subconscious and stifled my spiritual aspirations. Still, in my heart I knew I wanted to help people. Little did I know that a new disease was prowling through the shadows of the gay community in New York, and it would give me ample opportunity to help others.

AIDS – The Fear of Dying

It was the mid-80s in New York City, and the darkness known as AIDS was spreading—quickly. The theater and dance communities were losing talented artists by the day. The speed at which people were dying was overwhelming. Not only was there no cure, but there was also resistance to finding one due to the oppression faced by gay and lesbian individuals in our society. So many felt like it was God's way of punishing, even exterminating, gay men.

The 80s were for gay and lesbians what the 60s were for heterosexuals. Freedom, expression, and drug experimentation in the bars. They were a safe gathering place for a while. There was joy, and there was darkness. I cringed walking through the pitch black back rooms of the bars, whispering my friends' names who were having anonymous sex, telling them I was ready to go home. Before AIDS, gay men and lesbians were separated and there was tension. AIDS brought us together for the rights movement where lesbians took a leading role in activism.

We were so angry with the churches and government for their homophobia and not doing anything to help us. I joined ACT UP,[16] and we marched and laid down in Saint Patrick's Cathedral in protest. Protesting only heightened my anger and feeling of helplessness. I wanted to do something concrete to help.

A friend told me about this organization I could volunteer at, GMHC (Gay Men's Health Crisis).[17] I became a buddy team support group leader and witnessed the horrific effects of AIDS. The feeble men were skin and bones from their waists up and from their waists down severely swollen and disfigured from elephantiasis (ENV). I sat with many men covered in Kaposi sarcoma lesions, who struggled to breathe. I returned home in a panic, vigorously scrubbing my hands and body to make sure I didn't get "it."

My first Buddy client, Walter, lived in a tiny apartment stuffed with art. He was emaciated, and his voice quivered with fragility. When I arrived on my first day, his eyes lit up with joy. He was so lonely. Finally, he had someone to talk to, someone to listen to what he was dealing with, and for an hour each week, he mattered. His frail body couldn't lift anything anymore, and on each visit, I brought him groceries and essentials.

---

[16] The *AIDS Coalition to Unleash Power*, a grassroots activist organization formed in 1987 to advocate for people with HIV/AIDS and to promote awareness, treatment, and prevention of the disease.

[17] *GMHC* is a non-profit organization based in New York City that provides services and advocacy for people affected by HIV/AIDS, emphasizing education and wellness.

Walter had been an accomplished director of film and was an avid opera fan. To show his appreciation for the care I gave him, he invited me to the Metropolitan Opera House to see his favorite opera, *La Boheme*.[18] He whispered the details of the tragic storyline to me. I felt so much gratitude. My heart opened, and tears welled up in my eyes—it was my most intimate experience of compassion.

I attempted to hold it together for my clients, even though I was shivering inside. So many people were dying. My fear and overwhelm took a toll, and I began to isolate myself. I was losing hope—I was grappling with my mortality far too soon. My fear of dying from AIDS engulfed me, and the thought of witnessing one more person's death was unbearable. I experienced it all as an example of, "You will die if you are who you truly are." AIDS had such a stigma at the time that many people abandoned those who were afflicted for fear of contracting it—that and not being able to handle the gross physical manifestations they saw.

You Can Heal Your Body

Then, a colleague at GMHC introduced me to Louise Hay's[19] work. She was sharing her uplifting healing messages and insights with the AIDS community about how unexpressed trauma and emotions can be stored in specific areas of our bodies, leading to pain and illness. These were unfamiliar ideas to many people. Louise believed that self-love was the antidote to AIDS, that disease was a message from the body. Rather than looking outside for healing, she said, we should take responsibility for our health. Our emotions were the root cause and the true origin of illnesses.

---

[18] An opera composed by Giacomo Puccini, *La Boheme* is set in Paris and centered on the lives and loves of a group of struggling artists in the bohemian lifestyle of the 19th century.
[19] An influential American motivational author and the founder of Hay House, *Louise Hay* (1926–2017) is best known for her book *You Can Heal Your Life* (1984). In her work, she emphasizes the connection between mental patterns and physical health, advocating for self-love, affirmation, and positive thinking as tools for personal transformation and healing. Hay's teachings have inspired millions to explore the power of their thoughts and beliefs in shaping their realities.

She used affirmations to shift unexpressed emotions, pain, and disease into positive health and wellness. Her approach to wellness intrigued me.

Few people were exploring the impact of emotions, personal narrative—even ancestral trauma—on pain and disease in the body at that time. Louise's affirmation, "I listen with love to my body's messages"[20] felt empowering. I thought affirmations were something I could do to offset our fear of this virus.

Louise Hay, as we all now know, was right. The impact of our emotions on our bodies is now recognized through the psychosomatic roots of pain and illness.

I joined a community of individuals who were facing death and the stigma of AIDS. We faced similar struggles of what to do; how to help those living with AIDS and how to take care of ourselves, the caretakers, while witnessing so many deaths. Together we gathered in healing circles.

Many of us entered hunched over, our shoulders weighed down by the burdens we carried. As we meditated, chanted, shared our feelings, and prayed for healing, smiles returned to our faces, radiating a sense of wellbeing and renewed energy. Experiencing my transformation while witnessing it in others felt magical.

The tragedy of AIDS first terrified me, then enraged me. My anger turned to grief, and the fear remained—for years. I experienced the fear of dying at a very young age and on a huge scale. Being of service, sharing my compassion with people living with AIDS and their caregivers, made the horror a human experience for me. I was helping people in need of support. By encouraging people to not give up on life, I made a difference in their lives.

Additionally, in being part of the AIDS community, I was no longer alone in my fear and grief. I received the support I needed to keep showing

---

[20] Louise Hay, *You Can Heal Your Life* (Carlsbad, CA: Hay House, 1984), 125.

up. Isn't that what we are here for? Loving, supporting, and helping each other. Most of all, I connected with Spirit—the power that arises when people gather with a shared intention to heal and to open themselves to forces far greater than our human selves. It was my first taste of that, and I wanted more.

My intrigue propelled me to embark on a path of discovery. I was being introduced to new methods of accessing non-ordinary states, which felt more deeply rooted in me than my performances on stage did. I redirected my attention to exploring the religions and spiritual practices of the world. Living in New York City, a melting pot of cultures, made it easy to access a wide range of spiritual traditions. This is when my unique spiritual journey began.

In my next therapy session with Jackie, she asked me, "Have you met your spirit guide? She had taught me how to meditate by sending a grounding chord into the earth, so I wouldn't get lost in our explorations, but this was new.

Eager to meet my guide, I said "Yes!" After sending my chord down, she asked me to visualize a cloud and to ask for my guide to appear on it. Expecting an angel or a Buddha, I was surprised to see a tiny flamboyant man dressed in a sparkling sequined jacket approaching on a miniature horse.

"Honey," he playfully said, "I am Milton Sherman." His silly voice and words made me chuckle, and a lightness rose in my heart. I hadn't felt like that in a long time. After our introduction, he said, "Well...I have things to do." He waved and blew me a kiss as he said, "See you soon!" Then, he and his horse rode off into the void. I sunk back into the support of my chair and realized I now had another kind of support. Whenever I am feeling too serious or down, I call on Milton and within seconds, I smile and chuckle.

Emmanuel

After our session, Jackie told me about her friend Pat Rodegast, who channeled the spirit of *Emmanuel*.[21] She invited me to an event in a church on the Upper West Side. My mother had given me one of the *Seth*[22] books, channeled by Jane Roberts. Seth's main messages were based on the principle that consciousness creates matter, that we create our reality through our thoughts, feelings, and beliefs, and that our "point of power" is in the present moment.

I was familiar with the idea but had never heard a channeling session in person.

I entered the packed, bright sanctuary and sat at the back. I watched with curiosity as Pat closed her eyes and allowed Emmanuel's words to speak through her. Her countenance shifted etherically, and her voice timbre became warm and smooth as she spoke with a preciseness. Emmanuel's message was choosing love over fear. I wondered how she was connecting with Emmanuel. *Did she see him or hear him? What did she do within herself, with her body? Where was Emmanuel? Did he actually inhabit her body? Was Emmanuel male?* My questions were calmed by the words and their wisdom.

A warm glow of peace drifted and enveloped the sanctuary. I noticed bodies relaxing as they absorbed the wisdom Emmanuel was imparting. As the session completed, the woman sitting next to me turned and

---

[21] *Emmanuel* is a collection of channeled messages purportedly received from a spiritual entity, presented in books by Pat Rodegast and Judith Stanton, notably in *Emmanuel's Book* (1994). The teachings focus on themes of love, consciousness, and the spiritual journey, offering insights into the divine nature of humanity and promoting a deeper understanding of life's challenges from a spiritual perspective.

[22] *Seth* is a collection of spiritual teachings communicated by the medium Jane Roberts through a series of books and lectures, beginning with *Seth Speaks* (1972). These teachings explore metaphysical concepts such as the nature of reality, the multidimensional self, and the power of thoughts in shaping experience, emphasizing the interconnectedness of all existence and the potential for personal growth.

asked, "Are you going to the Harmonic Convergence tomorrow?" Since I lived a couple of blocks away from where the gathering was being held, Strawberry Fields, I knew I should go. Strawberry Fields is a garden in Central Park dedicated to John Lennon, a block from where he lived and was shot.

Harmonic Convergence

The Harmonic Convergence, held on August 16 and 17, 1987, was a globally synchronized peace meditation, coinciding with a rare alignment of the Sun, Moon, and six planets in our solar system. The timing was linked to a 5,125-year cycle in the Mayan calendar, suggesting a shift in consciousness.

It was a warm summer day in New York City, and I was greeted by the smell of incense burning as I entered the *Imagine* spiral. Tie dye shirts and dreadlocks all around. I have to admit at the time I didn't know how a global mediation could actually accomplish anything. I was still an activist, fighting for AIDS and gay rights. But I longed to promote peace and harmony.

As we prayed, chanted, and danced, I noticed a shift in my energy that soothed not only my body, but my mind. Through my shift in energy, I sensed the transformative power of my body moving in prayer. I wasn't dancing to feel good; I was moving with intention. *If that shifted my energy and those around me, could that actually ripple out beyond us?*

Afterwards, I continued to immerse myself in Louise Hay's affirmations and positive thinking techniques, which I still use today. However, I realized that shifting my mindset wasn't enough. My nervous system and body could not regulate or tolerate some of my feelings. Mind- and talk-based therapies changed my thinking, but it wasn't addressing my nervous system, so the awareness shifts weren't lasting.

I'd been experiencing a constant burning in my solar plexus, and I knew that it was because I wanted to numb my feelings and pretend that everything was great. My body was telling me something different. The more I ignored my body, the stronger my sensations and symptoms became. My body was not a comfortable place to be. It didn't feel safe to inhabit my body, so I chose not to. Before I'd had language or thoughts, I'd had intense feelings—and my body remembered them. My wounds of shame and grief were not just in my mind. They lived in my body and soul. They'd made imprints on my body. It was clear to me that when I'd left my body, my physical, mental, emotional, and spiritual pains had stayed embedded in my muscles and fascia. I struggled with sleepless nights and experienced panic attacks. My body was under constant stress, resulting in frequent cold sores. My symptoms were my body's way of communicating with me. I started to listen. I got help.

Massage

As a dancer, getting massages was essential for maintaining functionality and healing injuries. One of my friends from Stephens, Sarah, who had recently moved to New York, asked me to dance in a piece she was choreographing. I strained my hamstring during one rehearsal, and she told me about a couple of massage therapists who elevated functional massage through specialized techniques. Judith and Michael, a couple from Vermont, came to the city to provide massages. I had never had a session with two therapists before—one at my head, the other at my feet; one on my left, the other on my right. Their sessions calmed my nervous system and taught me the art of breathing and relaxation.

Their approach not only eased muscle and fascia tension and pain but also addressed the underlying emotions that often contributed to the discomfort. Gradually, I felt comfortable enough to unwind. This newfound connection with my body ignited a profound desire to deepen my understanding of these practices.

Judith and Michael invited Sarah and me to their charming colonial home in the picturesque Vermont countryside for a weekend breathwork retreat. Holotropic breathwork involves deep, rhythmic breathing for a few hours, accompanied by uplifting music. Initially, my body seemed to shut down, but as I breathed deeply, I surrendered to how these sensations wanted to move. Expressing my sensations authentically, I experienced profound releases not just physically but within my psyche and soul. The sense of freedom and lightness I felt in both body and mind was transcendent, and the deep peace and connection I experienced within myself and in others ignited my curiosity about this relatively new practice.

The course of my life was being redirected. My spiritual journey was gaining significance, and my interest in the body and healing was growing. I wanted to explore more in life beyond acting and dancing professionally. I felt a vibrant energy in my hands that yearned to move, express, and heal.

At that time, I was managing a restaurant in Lincoln Center to support myself between dancing and acting jobs. The waiters roller-skated through the restaurant, and even though it looked fun, it was stressful. One Halloween we all dressed in costume, me as the "Church Lady"—Dana Carvey's character from Saturday Night Live. In between greeting customers with the infamous phrase "Well...isn't that special?" with my lips pursed and a cock of my head, I started massaging the waiters' shoulders to relieve their stress. Soon, a line formed (apparently, I was good at massage!).

For the next month, I kept looking at my hands. I sensed a buzzing energy of light flowing through them. I knew I was supposed to do something with this energy, so I called Judith and Michael. They recommended the school where they trained, Heartwood Institute, isolated in the rolling hills of northern California. I applied and, with their recommendation, I was accepted easily. I gave my notice to the restaurant—they thought I was joining a cult.

Something larger and magical was guiding me on my path. It was time to leave New York and travel into the unknown. So I surrendered to this guidance and embarked on a new journey.

What does the voice of fear whisper to you?
Fear speaks to you in logic and reason.
It assumes the language of love itself,
Fear tells you "I want to make you safe."
*Love says, "You **are** safe."*
—Emmanuel

3

Safe to Feel

I sold what little furniture I had and said goodbye to New York. It was time. I spent a couple of weeks visiting my parents and familiarized myself with the Heartwood literature. The classes piqued my interest; they described new healing practices I had not heard of. The words love and harmony were used a lot. I liked that. The pictures in the magazine were beautiful—the mountains, the hot tub, and no one was dressed in designer clothes. But I was going alone. *Can I trust that this is my next step?* I had no idea what to expect or what I would find when I got there.

I had never been to San Francisco, but my parents had and they loved it. Dad shared his memories of Esalen Institute[23] at Big Sur, where he learned Gestalt therapy.[24] Ahead of his time, Dad basically had brought Gestalt to the Midwest. I gleamed while listening to him talk about his passion for helping others and started to get excited for my trip the next day.

Once we landed, I took a bus to the downtown station. I had a few hours to walk around before my next bus departed for Garberville, the town closest to Heartwood, a few hours north. San Francisco was magical. Its crazy hills and colorful Victorian architecture bathed in the warm

---

[23] The *Esalen Institute* is a holistic retreat center located in Big Sur, California, known for its emphasis on personal growth, bodywork, and spiritual practices, founded in the 1960s.
[24] *Gestalt Psychology:* A psychological approach emphasizing personal responsibility and the experience of the present moment, often used in psychotherapy to help individuals gain awareness of their thoughts, feelings, and behaviors as they relate to their environment.

California sun were intoxicating. San Francisco was the mecca of gay life in the 1980s, and I absorbed its laidback, "free" energy and sensual way of living. What a contrast from the serious, heavy, and darker feeling I experienced between the skyscrapers of New York City.

As the bus drove over the Golden Gate bridge, and the fog rolled in, caressing the lush green mountains that shot up out of the shiny blue Pacific Ocean, I had a mystical experience. I was met at the bus stop in Garberville by a young man with brown dreadlocks, a bright orange tie-dyed tank top, and Birkenstocks. His sparkling blue eyes greeted me, paired with a hug, as he said, "Welcome."

Dizzy with car sickness from the winding one-lane drive through the hills, I arrived at Heartwood, a secluded lodge where the air was filled with Joni Mitchell songs and a spirit of harmony. I was not in the city anymore. Nyra and Susanne met me at the lodge, dressed in flowing summer dresses, and attempted to orient my spinning.

Nyra's thin body masked her strength. Her long black hair, pulled back, accentuated her brown skin and deep dark brown eyes. She was of Puerto Rican and Dominican heritage. Her mother, Natividad, and I shared the same birthday with Mother Mary—septiembre ocho. Susanne's smile was so wide her eyes squinted as she boisterously laughed. Her laugh still echoes joyfully in my head. They took me inside the lodge for a light snack.

The earthy, organic food was grown on the land and blessed as it was cooked. *No meat, no coffee. How am I going to survive?* A lone payphone sat in a corner of the dining hall. That was my communication with the outside world for the next year. At first a shock for this city boy, this seclusion would be the perfect environment to reconnect with the earth, something that was desperately missing from my years living in the concrete jungle.

The rolling hills were full of redwoods. Summer was hot and dry. Close to the Pacific coast, from October to April it rained almost every day. There was a pack of huge domesticated pigs, turned wild, who roamed the hills and rooted the land. One of them was named Satan, whom I hoped to never meet. The people I met at Heartwood were so kind and loving. It was not only a school but a close-knit community.

At the communal gatherings we performed, danced, and chanted together. Nyra and Susanne, both from New York, loved it when I shared my "Church Lady" impersonation. Susanne begged me to perform at the next gathering, so we created "The Church Lady Show," where I interviewed guests. No more audition pressure, just pure fun and silliness.

Michelle was one of the women I interviewed. She was a staff member and artist. She invited me to her room for a shamanic journey. Drums, rattles, dream catchers, paints, and art supplies decorated her small dorm room. We sat down across from each other and meditated before she explained the purpose of a journey. She said we would enter a spiritual realm to receive guidance and insights from spirit beings. Michelle mentioned she sensed a side of me that I hid from others. A shadow.

I wondered what that was as I lay on the floor. The repetitive beats from her drum took me to an altered state of consciousness. I saw myself as a bird with a wide wingspan. My wings were sheltering little women who hid underneath them as fiery arrows from the sky pierced my wings. After the litany of attacks stopped, the little women came out and repaired the holes in my wings. This metaphor served as my first realization that my caretaker personality was accompanied by an unspoken expectation: I take care of you, and you reciprocate. It wasn't until later that I recognized the significant weight of the caretaker role I had been shouldering.

After the shamanic journey, together we made a mask, and Michelle and I performed my life's journey as a dance in front of the community a few days later. By moving my journey in performance, my body showed me how my belief that I was supposed to protect others affected the way I related to others energetically. So eager to fix others, I entered their energetic space without permission. When I did that, Michelle pulled away from me. The performance touched the audience. This would be my first experience of combining my extensive experience in the creative arts with the therapeutic process.

The therapeutic modality in the Transformational Therapy (TT) program integrated comprehensive massage training, polarity therapy, hypnotherapy, yoga, and the teachings of Gay and Katie Hendricks' method of transpersonal body-mind therapy. My neo-Reichian massage[25] training was designed to assist clients in releasing the emotional armor that we develop in our muscles and fascia from unexpressed emotions. Amy was my neo-Reichian teacher and co-lead the TT program with Richard, an older gay man whose focus was in counseling and hypnotherapy. Amy also taught the breathwork and Hendricks' method.

Doctors Gay and Katie Hendricks' method included affirmations integrated with educational kinesiology[26] movements like cross crawl[27] for full body-mind integration. I achieved altered states of consciousness, like bliss, when I discovered places in my body that were blocked, breathed into them, and expressed fully. This enhanced what I had learned from Louise Hay and was exactly what I was looking for. This process guided me deeper into my body and my emotional landscape.

---

[25] *Neo-Reichian Massage:* A therapeutic bodywork technique derived from the theories of Wilhelm Reich, focusing on the release of physical and emotional tension stored in the body. Developed by practitioners such as Alexander Lowen and John Pierrakos, Neo-Reichian massage combines elements of deep tissue massage, breathwork, and psychological awareness to promote healing and personal growth. It aims to help individuals access and integrate repressed emotions, facilitating a greater sense of well-being and connection to the body.

[26] *Educational Kinesiology* is a method that uses physical movement and exercises to enhance learning, improve cognitive function, and address learning disabilities.

[27] *Cross Crawl:* A movement practice that involves alternating arm and leg movements to engage both hemispheres of the brain, often used in educational kinesiology to support coordination and cognitive integration.

Gay, along with Stanislav Grof, brought breathwork into the culture in the 1970s and 80s. Katie enhanced their method, weaving in her movement background. These modalities were new to most people at that time, and when they arrived for a two week intensive, I learned the foundation of my personal and professional practices. Gay's books, *Learning to Love Yourself* and *Conscious Breathing* became staples in my body-mind practice and how I would help others.

Conscious breathing is the most essential and beneficial practice I have learned. Most of us were taught to inhale into our lungs. This actually stimulates the fight or flight response—feeding anxiety and fear. The premise of conscious breathing is to inhale into a relaxed diaphragm, allowing it to gently inflate and eventually fill the lungs. This way of breathing relaxes our nervous systems, calming our feelings and thoughts. By calming our thoughts, we can more easily inhabit the present moment and sense our internal experience.

Gay and Kathlyn's book *Conscious Loving* was way ahead of its time, detailing their concept of "speaking the truth of your internal experience as you are perceiving it" in a relationship.

In the 80s in California, we were experimenting with these new methods in an environment of freedom from societal norms; there was a lack of healthy boundaries. We pushed and forced releases that often exposed and re-traumatized some people. Several had breakdowns. Some disappeared. There weren't anchors and safety measures present, and this eventually led to stricter safety measures in licensing of therapies.

The community was in grief, and Amy was struggling with her grief the most, as the leader of the Native American church, Rutherford, her spiritual father, had died in a car accident the day before I arrived. She and Michelle invited me to a sweat lodge that was held down the hill from my room. Little did I know how meaningful this experience would be. I would find anchors and safety in practices of the Native American church that many members of the Heartwood community participated in.

As I walked down the path to the lodge, a gentle breeze whispered a sacred message, "This is your home." As I turned the corner, a fierce fire burned over a pit in the dirt. Under the fire were large round glowing rocks. Hours before entering the lodge, the fire is lit, heating the rocks that will purify those taking part in the ceremony.

The Power of the Circle

We all stood in silence around the fire, waiting for Chief Calvin Magpie to arrive. As his truck pulled up, I didn't know what to expect. He jumped out his truck, laughing as he approached. Calvin was a stout Cherokee/Arapahoe man who chuckled at every opportunity. His chuckle was sacred. It brought lightness to those who were in pain. "Are you ready?" he said. I wasn't sure if I was.

The twenty of us squeezed into this small dome of blankets supported by willow branches. The fiery rocks were brought in and placed in a hole in the center, and water was poured on them, creating steam so hot, it scalded my skin. In a breathwork session, I felt a connection to a field of loving spaciousness. But what I was about to experience was mind-boggling.

Inside the dark, cramped space, the heat strips away all pretenses, leaving only the raw truth. It dissolves everything that is false. If I am resisting forgiveness, for example, the heat will make it intolerable. I might have difficulty breathing and will want to get out. But the rule of the sweat lodge is that no one leaves before the ceremony is complete. So, you have to deal with what is coming up and allow the emotions to release. I was learning to develop the capacity to stay with and trust the process until a shift had occurred—to be with others' pains and struggles with steadfast compassion.

I allowed judgments to die in the lodge; I shed aspects of myself that weren't aligned with my soul.

Parts of me died in the heat, and as I exited the lodge after the ceremony, others were born. The circle of ceremony is a group experience where everyone not only matters, but our personal prayers turn into global concerns. I found safety in the protective environment of the lodge, the circle, and the reference points, and anchors provided by the ritual—with the songs, prayers, and elements of fire, water, earth, and air—held me fully.

The prayers and songs anchored a collective reverence for Great Spirit. The anchors—the fire, the rocks, and the water focused my mind when it wanted to wonder. They kept me present. The community provided a container of support that I didn't feel as deeply in classes or sessions, and staying until the ceremony was over also supported safety for me.

"All my relations" is always exclaimed when the door opens after a round. It is a phrase used by indigenous peoples in North America to express their belief in the interconnectedness of all beings. It conveys the idea that everyone and everything has a place in the world and that we maintain balance and harmony with each other, the land, the air, the water, and the Universe.

The enormous spaciousness I experienced after sharing the cramped space, covered in mud, was the first place I connected with Great Spirit in community. When I returned to my body, I shifted from being led by my head to being guided by my heart.

The sweat lodge is a powerful vehicle that supports the experience of unity. It is founded on an intention for prayer, the first of many reference points. This intention starts the process and gathers people together with a common focus or point of convergence. Each person confronts their personal limits, but with the support of the group, the intention, and reference points, the ceremony ends in a renewed celebration of this life and honors everyone's piece of the puzzle. It was my first glimpse of understanding that I didn't need to, or, rather, can't do this life alone.

This sweat lodge experience evolved into a spiritual practice for me. Since I had not yet cultivated the resilience to embrace these blessings independently, I returned to this sacred space frequently to absorb its invaluable wisdom. The components of this ceremonial ritual encompassed intention, anchors, and the amplification that supports the release of what no longer serves us. Rooted in ancient wisdom, these elements served as the original foundation for the transpersonal somatic work I was studying.

As my program was coming to an end, Mom told me there was a massage position open at a massage center her friend worked at. I knew she wanted me to come "home." Since I was also excited to have a job right after graduating, I was happy to head back to my hometown.

After my last sweat lodge, I prayed for a loving relationship with a beautiful man. I wrote all of the qualities I was looking for and ended up forgetting one.

As I was leaving, Calvin said to me, "Remember the sweat lodge when you get home. The world can try and make you forget. Call on your memories. We are here for you always."

I learned so much in the secluded safety of Heartwood. The teachings and people I met have stayed in my heart. I believed I was going to Heartwood to just learn massage and somatic therapy,[28] but the sacred Native American practices opened me up to my deeper roots in ancient indigenous wisdom.

---

[28] *Somatic therapy* refers to a form of body-centered therapy that integrates the connection of mind and body in the healing process. See *Psychology Today*, s.v. "Somatic Therapy," accessed September 1, 2025, https://www.psychologytoday.com/us/therapy-types/somatic-therapy.

The Power of Releasing

When I returned back to Columbia, I met with the owner of the Swedish Massage Center and was hired on the spot. My mom had shared her books with me in the past, so I brought one for her that many women at Heartwood found empowering, *The Courage to Heal.*[29]

A month later, I asked her if she found it helpful. She replied, "I had to put it down after the first chapter. I couldn't breathe." Her statement confirmed an intuitive hunch I had ever since I was young. *Something bad had happened to her too.*

After working at the Swedish Massage Center for a few months, I opened my own office. The private space allowed me to integrate more of my transformational skills in sessions with my massage clients—creating a place they felt safe to feel more deeply. This was when I freelanced with Doc Kim and recovered the memory I began this book with. In both of these healing environments, my senses heightened. As I witnessed firsthand how trapped emotions manifested in each of my clients' bodies, affecting their muscles, organs, and fascia, I began supporting them in breathing deeply and expressing these emotions fully.

The truth of how beneficial releasing caged anger can be came to the fore for me when I worked with my client Kathleen. During our first session, as I was massaging her mid back, she started to weep. She revealed her breast cancer diagnosis. And when she turned over on her back, she showed me the scars from her recent breast cancer surgery. As she continued crying, a deep bond between us developed. During our next session, she connected to a profound pain in her heart. I guided her to breathe into her

---

[29] *The Courage to Heal* is a seminal self-help book authored by Ellen Bass and Laura Davis, first published in 1988, that addresses the healing process for survivors of childhood sexual abuse. The book combines personal narratives, practical exercises, and therapeutic insights, empowering readers to confront their trauma, reclaim their lives, and foster healing through community and support. It has been influential in shaping conversations around sexual abuse and recovery.

chest, encouraging her pain to discover its own movement and expression. Intense rage emerged, causing her hands to ball into fists and her jaw to clench. A scream escaped her, and I supported her in expressing herself. As she shook her head and body, a memory of past sexual abuse resurfaced and she screamed, "No!"

After her release, she sank to the floor. Her body softened, and a warm, pink glow rose in her face. Her breath deepened, and she told me she felt a deep sense of peace. By amplifying her breathing and moving, a release—physical and emotional—occurred. When her breath amplified what she was feeling, she brought consciousness to an unconscious feeling. As she amplified her breathing and movement, it became more difficult to resist her mind and body's impulses to release what her body and mind no longer wanted to tolerate.

We continued our sessions for several months, and I saw the harm unexpressed anger causes physically and emotionally. It can be the root of much pain and many illnesses. Saying "No" to past trauma is an empowering stance. The ability to say no is a trait of long-term survivors; the ability to communicate. (A couple of years after we worked together, Kathleen contacted me to share that her cancer remained in remission.) This experience illuminated the profound impact of our work, deeply emphasizing not only the healing that occurs but also the enduring impact of freeing suppressed emotions. Additionally, it showcased the strength found in saying "Yes" to life and embracing the support that comes our way.

My experience with Kathleen inspired me to return to volunteering to support people living with AIDS. I led a support group at the Mid-Missouri AIDS Project. My mom's friend Sharon called and told her about the AIDS Medicine and Miracles conference in Boulder, Colorado. Dr. Bernie Siegel and Marianne Williamson co-founded this event as a forum to present alternative healing approaches for people living with AIDS. Sharon had moved to Boulder and offered for me and a couple of my group members to stay with her.

A couple of weeks later, the three of us and our bags packed into my two-door Volkswagen Scirocco and drove through the plains of Kansas to Boulder. Tim was a boisterous twenty-seven-year-old former hairdresser. He was a tall and thin man with small lesions who had just lost his partner. Terry was a shy young man of twenty-five years. He had developed pneumocystis pneumonia. The medications at the time were not helping them, and they both were eager to find alternative solutions to their physical and emotional pain. They were looking for hope.

When we arrived, Sharon gave me a bear hug, embracing me like she would her favorite animal. Her home in Boulder was breathtaking, with the iconic Flatirons jutting out from the foothills of the Front Range of the Rockies.

As the guys settled into their rooms, Sharon and I reminisced about my childhood. She took care of my brother, sister, and me when my parents travelled. We played games like "Capture the Flag." She was so creative and playful with us. Her parents and Grandpa Harland and Grandma Tommie were close friends. We are family. It was great to reconnect with her playful spirit and generous heart.

The next morning, we arrived at the conference. I was used to the heartfelt atmosphere, but it was new for my group members. The conference had loads of holistic resources they had not been exposed to. One of the classes was simply laughing—revealing the healing power that laughter has on our bodies and minds. The guys flirted and had warm connections with other men from around the country. My heart warmed seeing their smiles as they discovered empowering ways to live, even in the midst of such devastating life situations.

Tim and Terry didn't want to leave, but the next morning we crammed into an even tighter car with our hearts expanded for the ten-hour drive back to Columbia.

The morning after we returned, my friend Nyra from Heartwood called. We hadn't talked since I left Heartwood. She told me she met someone at a wheatgrass juicing retreat that she thought I should meet. His name was Eli Hollingworth. *So elegant*, I thought. She gave me Eli's number, and I called him. We fell in love over the phone. He flirted and wrote me dreamy love poems. As a hopeless romantic, his words hooked me.

Eli invited me to Chicago to meet him. When he picked me up at the airport, I was stunned by his handsome chiseled face and crystal blue eyes. He drove me to his lavish apartment, where I was greeted by Barrington, his Great Dane. He had tickets to the *Oprah* show. We went to Unity church, and he knew everyone there. The next day, we visited his mother in Kohler, Wisconsin, a charming village where everyone works for Kohler. His mother loved me immediately.

This was all happening so fast.

The next day, I helped him plant flowers in his garden and I developed a headache in the sun. I asked if he had an aspirin, and he said he did in his medicine cabinet. As I opened the door, I saw two bottles next to the aspirin and recognized they were HIV medications. I froze. I needed to come down from my love high and deal with this reality. I had to be safe. I wondered why he hadn't told me.

I was leaving for home the next day, and we were going out dancing that night. Several guys at the club were hitting on me. Eli became jealous and told me we had to leave. When we returned back to his place, the tension between us was palpable. I asked him why he hadn't told me about being HIV positive, and he broke into tears. "Because I thought you wouldn't love me."

We laid there in silence, and I held his hand. I didn't think I could risk losing another friend.

When I returned to Columbia, I received a call telling me KC had died. Another dear friend, Terry, died a few days later.

I was distraught, losing two of my best friends and finding out Eli was HIV positive. I believed I would never have love in my life. I spiraled into a deep depression. At twenty-nine, I was too young for this to be happening, and no one in my life knew what I was going through.

Unexpectedly, Amy gave me a call and said she needed an assistant. She was wondering if I wanted to come back to Heartwood and work. It was a gift from Great Spirit. "Of course," I said. I packed my Scirocco and I returned to Heartwood to both work on the staff and teach. I taught a movement class where we explored breathing and movement.

Working at Heartwood was not as joyous as being a student. I was not a sales master, and one of my jobs was to attract students for intensives. Returning to the sweat lodge and the Native American ways, however, was a homecoming for me that I had missed.

There was a woman on the grounds crew, Brenda. She had more masculine energy than I did, and we connected in the sweat lodge. She made drums. One day, Brenda asked me if she could make a drum for me and I was elated.

A few days later, Brenda handed me the light brown deerskin drum. The skin was soft, stretched taut and tied in the back. When I beat it with the mallet, the beats reverberated with the healing tones I remembered from my session with Michelle.

Michelle was no longer teaching at Heartwood, and I was teaching a movement class. The teaching side of my role allowed me to explore combining breath and movement, and that was a blessing. With my new drum in hand for one class, I began exploring drumming while the group was moving. After that class, I had the idea of combining a shamanic journey with movement afterwards to support the integration of the experience.

I presented my idea to Heartwood, and they supported me in leading my first group during a weekend break from regular classes. A gathering of the Billy Club, a Northern California group of rural gay men, many of whom were living with AIDS, was being held at Heartwood. After the journey, I played music for the movement to integrate, and as the guys moved, everyone started taking off their clothes. As I watched this unfold, I pretended to be comfortable with their freedom, feeling a bit shocked on the inside, wondering how this would play out.

Eventually, the men began hugging, which led to cuddling on the floor, and I gently guided them to form a circle and share about their experiences. Many spoke of how the drum beats and their journey connected them with their warrior-like energy and gave them a sense of power in the face of living with AIDS.

While challenging to facilitate at first, this group became an exercise in creating safety and allowing the unfolding. It also inspired me to submit an application to present this workshop at the next AIDS Medicine and Miracles conference, in Boulder, Colorado. My application was accepted, and I called my workshop the *Inner Warrior:*

This workshop begins with a discussion of warriorism. To contact the inner warrior you are led on a shamanic journey—a dream-like hypnotic journey inward guided by Native American drumming. After the journey is completed, you will move or dance from your inner experiences. Then you will move together with others in what is called contact improvisation dance. One theme that surfaces through this event is the development of the ability to stay connected to one's power while in direct contact with others, or in this case with HIV. This can be extremely beneficial in creating more inner strength, guidance, and healing in oneself.

Being in Boulder rekindled my love for Colorado. The participants were gleaming afterwards and thanked me for creating the space for them to access a sense of power in facing hopelessness. I gleamed, as well, from how this experience helped them persevere. My creation had really helped people. But I didn't feel quite worthy of beating my drum. The workshop was a wonderful creation with well-meaning intention, but I felt like an imposter beating the drum. It would take many years to feel worthy.

When I returned to Heartwood after the conference, I came across an advertisement for the Master's Degree program in Somatic Psychology,[30] specializing in Dance and Movement Therapy at the Naropa Institute (now Naropa University) Since Katie Hendricks co-founded the program, I knew I wanted to learn more and receive the credential. I applied and was provisionally accepted. An in-person audition was required, but I was told my background with the Hendricks work made my acceptance almost assured. I called Sharon to tell her the news, and she said, "You can stay with me until you start your program." So I loaded up my silver Volkswagen Scirocco and set off on the lengthy journey through the desert to the Rocky Mountains and Boulder, Colorado.

Arriving in the snow and cold of January, Sharon welcomed me with a nice cup of hot tea, and we began our months of supporting each other. I felt so grateful to have her support during my transition. As she got me settled in my room, Sharon shared that she was grieving a breakup and was experiencing challenges with her work. I listened and supported her through her emotional pains. She supported me with her generosity, treating me to skiing almost every weekend. I wasn't very good, but I relished in the view from the top. There is nothing quite like the contrast of the pure white snow and the brilliant blue Colorado sky on a sunny day. Mountains speak to me—it's like I am closer to Spirit.

---

[30] *Somatic Psychology:* A therapeutic approach that emphasizes the connection between the mind and body, focusing on bodily sensations and experiences as integral to understanding psychological issues and promoting healing.

I had nine months to acclimate to Boulder and find a job so I could rent an apartment before my program commenced in September.

One summer day, as I was helping Sharon build a fence and dodging her "you hammer like a girl" pokes, out of the blue, Eli called. He said he was coming to Boulder to meet Hanna Kroeger, a controversial woman who gave healings at her Chapel of the Miracles. He had heard she could heal persons living with AIDS. When I picked him up at the airport, I couldn't believe what I saw. His once-handsome face was hollowed—Eli looked like he was eighty years old. We were only thirty-three.

I drove Eli to the Chapel in the countryside. When we arrived, a long line had already formed outside, waiting for this tiny, elderly woman wearing an Amish-like dress to heal them. I stood next to Eli, and when it was his turn, he met with her for just a few seconds before she lowered her head and said, "I am sorry. There is nothing I can do." Devastated, I watched Eli's hopes vanish. I did my best to comfort him as we drove back to Sharon's house. He criticized my driving all the way back, attempting to control anything he could.

A few weeks later, Eli's mother called to inform me of his passing. Again, I felt devastated; I wasn't sure how I would cope if another person were to die. I funneled my grief into service again. Sharon knew the director of BCAP, the Boulder County AIDS Project, and introduced me to Tim. I led a weekly support group, and one day, Tim invited me to their summer picnic.

As he introduced me to the gay men of Boulder, I locked eyes with Tom. It was love at first sight. He stood tall but leaned in to speak, his skin a rich shade of dark brown. Though shy and reserved, I could sense his attraction toward me. I hadn't felt such a spark. It was grounded and calm. Despite being twelve years older, his skin was soft and barely aged more than mine.

On our first date, we talked for hours. Tom was a sergeant for the sheriffs department and worked at the county jail. He didn't like the job, but it provided him with a nice lifestyle. We had so many common loves, connecting deeply through our favorite singers; the incomparable voices of Patti Labelle and Luther Vandross. I shared with him the kind of "conscious loving" relationship I desired, and he said, "I'm not sure I can do that."

I said, "Sure you can!" I didn't listen to him.

He was the man I had prayed for at the sweat lodge, and I had left out one thing—deep intimacy.

On our second date, he drove me to his new house that was being built. When we got back in his black Acura, he told me to fasten my seatbelt by saying, "I don't want anything to ever happen to you." He would say that every time we got in his car.

A couple months later, he invited me to live with him.

My mother called one day to inform me that Grandmother Tommie needed to move to managed care and asked if I wanted her cat, Harry. I had never had a cat, so asked Tom, and he surprised me by saying yes. I flew back to pick up Harry. When we returned, I showed Harry his litter box in the basement. After a day of hiding in the basement, Harry came to the second floor and slept with us on the bed. The next morning, on our way downstairs, he jumped off the staircase, flew through the air, and landed on his feet on the sofa in the living room. He loved his big new home. Tom affectionately called Harry "Hair."

Meditation

My two-year master's program began. Naropa had the feel and smell of Heartwood, but with more brick and mortar and a Tibetan Buddhist twist. My studies at Naropa University exposed me not only to somatic psychology but also to Buddhist meditation practices.

Meditation is the practice of developing awareness without attachment in the present moment. Awareness is much bigger than the thinking mind.

Contemplative and mindfulness meditation practice was the cornerstone of Naropa. Contemplative meditation is a practice that involves focused thinking and reflection on a specific subject or concept, allowing the mind to explore its depths without necessarily reaching a conclusion. It differs from mindfulness, which emphasizes non-judgmental awareness of the present moment. In contemplative meditation, the mind engages with a chosen topic, but it's a guided exploration rather than a detached observation.

Tonglen, or "taking and giving" is a meditation practice that combines meditating on loving-kindness with meditating on compassion. You imagine taking in others' suffering as dark smoke and giving all that they need as bright light.

At first, sitting on a zafu, spine straight, in silence, seemed impossible. I tried to observe my thoughts and let them pass, but my mind raced. I brewed over all the things I needed to do afterward, what the other people sitting with me were thinking, and how I looked. My body tensed from sitting. My first realization was, *Wow. I have a lot of thoughts.* I was so attached to them.

I was intrigued by a Tibetan Buddhist practice known as the Rainbow Body, in which practitioners dissolve the body and mind into light at the moment of death, and for some, even during life.

I learned to develop "my witness" or "the observer" of my inner world of thoughts, feelings, and bodily sensations. Developing my inner awareness as a witness who could recognize and distinguish my feelings from thoughts opened my eyes to my inner landscape, and at first, it was overwhelming. I saw many aspects of myself that I didn't want to see—and didn't want to own.

My dance career taught me to reach through and past my fingertips and toes to create lines and full movement sequences. I learned to feel my body, sense my balance, and project the emotions of the dance to the audience with my body. The movement therapy I was learning at Naropa taught me that when we experience traumatic events, our movement or expression is first jarred and then stopped, and we cannot allow the movement to discharge through our bodies. As our movement is stifled, the unexpressed emotion from the traumatic event becomes logged and stuck in our bodies.

Have you ever interrupted a cat when they are starting to stretch or jump? They must start the stretch over and complete that action. Harry was a wonderful teacher for me—if I picked him up mid-stretch, before he could stretch fully, I witnessed Harry's innate persistence to complete the sequence I interrupted. When I released him, I observed upon finishing his movement, Harry radiated a sense of freedom and peace.

It is such a lesson for us humans to follow our inner guidance to free stuck energy from our bodies, minds, and souls. By completing a movement, our body can unwind the stuck tension, and the unexpressed emotion can move through fully. Its expression is a release of excess energy. This release keeps us open and receptive to the flow of life.

My instructors taught their personal movement methods: Christine Caldwell taught the Moving Cycle—a circular method that moves from awareness, acceptance, and owning to action.

Christine introduced her students to the work of Focusing,[31] developing our "felt sense,"[32] and Susan Aposhyan taught her work, body-

---

[31] Eugene T. Gendlin, *Focusing* (New York: Bantam Books, 1981). Gendlin's book introduces a psychotherapeutic self-help method that teaches individuals how to tap into their "felt sense," a bodily awareness that guides emotional healing and personal growth.

[32] *Felt Sense:* A sensory and emotional awareness of bodily states, often described in somatic psychology as a way to access deeper feelings and insights about one's experiences.

mind psychotherapy,[33] introducing Bonnie Bainbridge Cohen's Body-Mind Centering.[34]

Susan taught me to more deeply sense my body parts and how to access my body's wisdom by feeling these parts. Christine taught me the power of going within my body and developing the courage to know where the process would take me. Authentic movement taught me to explore the unconscious through self-directed movement. All of their teachings supported the deep awareness of the body's sensations and emotions, enhanced self-awareness and compassion, and supported greater resilience.

I know that the amazing modalities that I learned in my master's program and approach to full-body awareness helped me to move past my childhood wounds I had been carrying with me through my whole adult life. Applying these principles to my own life helped me to heal, move forward, and live my dreams.

My studies and degree in somatic psychology have fostered a reverence for my body as an amazing, self-healing instrument whose systems are always moving toward wellbeing and balance. Every system in my body is designed to create health. My energy body wants to cleanse; my immune system seeks to protect me. The body is trying to release that which does not belong inside all the time. On the other hand, the mind and ego want to control how we think we want things to be.

Mindset is the result of how our mind and ego work together to create our internal narrative. The mind wants control, and the ego reinforces

---

[33] *Body-Mind Psychotherapy (BMP)* is a somatic approach to psychotherapy based heavily on Body-Mind Centering, developed in the 80s by Susan Aposhyan. BMP 2.0 added trauma-awareness and circular attunement. Now BMP 3.0 adds a recognition that each of our spirituality is inherent in our embodiment and that these times require that we all learn to work with ourselves and others.

[34] *Mind-Body Centering:* A somatic practice that combines movement, touch, and awareness to explore the connections between the body and mind, often used in dance and therapy settings to enhance body awareness and expression.

patterns that feel familiar or safe—even if they're limiting. Shifting our mindset is a powerful and advanced practice, but it's not just about repeating affirmations or thinking positively. If we don't clear the negative thoughts and emotions stored in the body, they linger and continue to influence us beneath the surface. True mindset work involves not just changing thoughts but also moving and releasing what's stuck in the body.

When we hold on to emotions or thoughts, they become embedded in our bodies, and we block the flow of life, meaning our energy and balance.

All feelings are meant to be expressed. When we allow ourselves to express what we feel—through movement, voice, and truthful communication—we support the natural flow of presence through our bodies. In somatic psychology, presence refers to our ability to be fully aware and attuned to our moment-to-moment experience, creating coherence between the mind and body. Suppressing feelings disrupts this flow and can have both psychological and physical health consequences. In every life experience, we are given a choice: to engage fully with what's happening, or to withdraw. Expression—whether through physical movement or honest acknowledgment of our emotional and physical state—is what keeps us connected, alive, and present.

When we try to suppress our thoughts and feelings, they don't go away—they become more activated. The internal contraction creates pressure, and the natural desire or need to express gets shunted. That resistance actually intensifies the emotion, making it demand our attention even more. The more we push it down, the more it builds up beneath the surface. Despite our attempts to numb or distract ourselves, unprocessed emotions don't disappear—they build up and get louder. Then they can manifest as chronic pain, illness, and disease. This new awareness further echoed and expanded upon my early exposure to Louise Hay.

Integrating Theater, Dance, and Therapy

The requirements of my graduate program at Naropa included two internships. My first internship was at a locked psychiatric hospital. I cringed every time the steel door slammed behind me when I entered to lead my groups. One night in bed with Tom, after a couple of months working there, I gasped and screamed, bolting out of bed. I told Tom, "One of my clients was peeling her skin off, and I was running down the hall as my group was screaming and chasing me."

He said firmly, "Tomorrow is your last day there." Tom knew what I was experiencing, as he was exposed to the same disturbing behavior at the jail each day.

At Naropa, the coursework was rigorous and I, like many of the students, pushed myself too hard. I worked every night at a restaurant to support myself. I was still smoking and I rarely rested. With all of the stress, I developed a type of vertigo, which I later discovered was caused by stress and an overactive spleen (the worry organ in Chinese medicine). I couldn't stand up without fear of falling, so I tensed every muscle in my body to keep myself upright. I would lean on a wall or hold on to the tables of the restaurant to stabilize myself as I took the customers' orders and delivered their meals. My breathing was shallow and labored. I was disconnected from my body. I couldn't "hold it all together."

A part of me believed that smoking was relaxing me, yet deep down, my soul recognized it was adding to my stress, in how I perceived myself and how I wished to be perceived by others. In my incoherence, I drenched myself in cologne to mask the scent of cigarettes. Everyone was aware I was hiding something, even if they didn't acknowledge it. My shame felt burdensome. Although I was learning various healing techniques in my studies and released past wounds, when I returned home, they would resurface, leaving me feeling powerless. My shame was keeping me incoherent and holding my inner child[35] heart at bay.

---

[35] *Inner child* refers to the part of the psyche that retains childlike aspects of personality, emotions, and unmet developmental needs; it is often explored in psychotherapy to

My program also required writing a thesis, which I embellished with a performance project. My thesis, "Dance/Movement Therapy: A Vital Adjunctive Treatment for Persons Living with AIDS: A Catalyst for Change," centered on my deep belief that disease can be healed through emotional release and creative expression. My second internship was at the Colorado AIDS Project, where I created a movement therapy group for five male clients called the Discovery Group. I combined my professional theater and dance training, my experience at Heartwood of blending performance with the therapeutic process, and my grief from losing so many friends to AIDS. Our journey together through music, movement, voice, and the written word culminated in a performance of their experience *Fluid: Sharing Our Conversations with AIDS*.

FLUID: Sharing Our Conversations with AIDS

The performance space at Denver's Mercury Cafe was packed as these men courageously exposed their pain and healing. As the other performers moved, cried, and shouted their anger, Christopher read his poem he wrote in our class.

Floating:

> *I throw—the healing energy protects me*
> *I throw—the healing energy encircles me*
> *I throw—the healing energy engulfs me...*
> *swallows me...whole*
> *And I patiently float in the blue green Fluid*
> *And it is so still that I have started forgetting the boundaries of my body*
> *Where do I start? Where does it connect?*
> *And this darkness inside my veins has brought light to certain blacked areas of my brain*

---

access healing from early trauma. See John Bradshaw, *Homecoming: Reclaiming and Championing Your Inner Child* (New York: Bantam Books, 1990).

The gray matters The gray......matters
Suspending liquid keeps me afloat and away...island like
All I can see is up
Colors all around me:
Orange, blue, red, green, black, yellow
Shift... Swirling... swimming
All I imagine beneath me is murky thick gray
As I still lie suspended in healing and patiently float
Trying not to be sucked under
by the monsters in the dark underneath
Trying not to panic... PANIC leads to drowning
Overwhelming swallowing
All of the imaginary dark
So I patiently float with focus above
The dark gray whose surface I float on
This blackness which swarms within
Holds me up, Pulls me down
And if I let it be and be with it... I'll live
And if the thoughts it begins consume my mind...
It can kill me
But one thing remains certain...It Is Me...

Tears filled the room. Many in the audience were personally facing the harsh reality of AIDS. It was 1995, and many people continued to die at alarming rates. I still find myself in tears when I read "Floating." Its truth resonates with me on a deep level. At that moment, I recognized the powerful effect of sharing our stories. The event offered healing to everyone present, breaking down the barriers between performer and audience.

My belief that it was possible to heal through expression and performance, which I wrote about in my thesis, was still a lofty idea for most people, as they were still completely reliant on modern medicine. I don't know if any of the men's life expectancies lengthened, but they connected to their souls. They healed many of the ways AIDS affected them, and that gave them a sense of power to live more fully in the face of what was, for most of them, a helpless situation. This collective healing experience became the peak experience of my graduate school journey. It was the manifestation of my vision outlined in my thesis. I wondered what could be possible through the healing power of sacred artistic expression with large groups of people like I experienced at the Harmonic Convergence.

After graduating, I accepted the administration position for our department. The faculty and staff of Naropa were invited to a private sitting with the Dalai Lama at the Oxford Hotel in Denver. It was my first authentic experience of feeling a human being's frequency radiating. As he exited the room, we all bowed and were instructed to be lower than him. As he passed by me, a swoosh of cool energy wafted over me and I broke into tears. I was transported deep within my sacred heart. He embodies compassion so fully that it radiates from him with an intensity that heals and transforms everyone around him. This was the highlight of my time in Boulder.

Exposed

Returning home, my relationship with Tom was unraveling. We loved each other so much but were rarely sexual, both still afraid of AIDS. Both of our best friends died recently. Every attempt to look in his eyes was met with a vacant gaze—a protection from seeing the depths of his soul, which I wanted more than anything.

He told me he couldn't, and I didn't listen.

Knowing a deep, soul-level relationship was not in the cards, I started pulling away from him emotionally and energetically. Knowing I had already left, he turned to me one night and said, "I think it's best that we separate." Tom left for a few days, not telling me where he was. Crushed and heartbroken, I spiraled. I behaved in ways I was not proud of. When Tom returned, I said, "Where were you?" to which he replied, " I needed to lick my wounds." Tom's parting words were "Take care of Hair. He's very special." I never saw him again.

Mutual friends invited me to stay with them while I searched for an apartment. Tom took care of Harry. After securing my new place, I went to pick up Harry, and Tom was in the shower. There were no parting words for me.

When I told Mom, she said, "What did you do?" *Not, are you OK?* My parents and Tom loved each other, and we all thought he was "the One."

The stress of realizing my relationship was over sent me into a helpless place. Alone, I spiraled into looking at erotic images of men again, this time on computers. It was the early 1990s, and computers were relatively new. There were all of these new sources for photos that one could endlessly fixate on. The network pulled me in, and when I would go to work at night, I would use the computer to view them. Naively, I didn't realize that those images were saved on the computer. The administrator of our department reported in one of our staff meetings she kept seeing these sensual images on her computer and they disturbed her. She reported it to the tech manager of the Institute, and he peered through a window one night and saw me. My secret had been exposed publicly. Mortified, I decided to resign.

The saving grace in this experience was that Susan came to me with no judgment, only love, and said, "I was just surprised that you would objectify people. That doesn't seem like you." She was right; it wasn't a side I presented to others, but it was a part of me. Endless searching for the perfect man, choosing images and bodies over connection.

Gay men are often perceived as depraved. My generation missed out on having intimate love connections in our adolescence. We had to hide and weren't able to date, thus our desires at that formative time were not able to connect with our hearts. We connected through fantasy, in dark rooms so no one could see. I was always uncomfortable with the anonymous and even multiple-partner sex some of us participate in. I desired a one-on-one connection, and Susan's statement really made me see what I was doing. I wasn't perverse; I was just looking for love and strength outside of myself.

After leaving Naropa, I struggled to make it on my own. One afternoon, while staring at the ceiling in my new apartment, panic set in as I realized I didn't have enough money to do my laundry. My sacrum locked up, and thoughts of desperation swirled. Then, I remembered I had Sharon's code to enter her home. Jumping into my car, I quickly drove over and quietly snuck into her place. I watched the clock the whole time. Just as I was transferring my clothes from the dryer to my bag, the back door swung open—Sharon had returned. I was caught once again. Puzzled, Sharon said, "What are you doing here?" Frozen in place, I couldn't look her in the eyes and frantically searched for an excuse to conceal my true reason for being there. I made up a silly excuse and said, "I gotta run."

This incident created a tension between us that lingered for years.

When I returned to my apartment, I beat myself up. Sharon held significant importance in my life, and I knew I had let her down. *Why didn't I just call her and ask?* Masking my shame was more important than being honest. In hindsight, I recognize that these experiences were my soul's way of signaling that I needed to change or I risked falling into a very dark place.

It was becoming clear that I needed others to take care of me and in return I gave them support emotionally. But my inner turmoil was showing me I really needed emotional support too. I understood my transformation was necessary. I was in a loop that I didn't know how to exit.

The Universe answered my prayer, and the next night I learned about a gay men's spirituality gathering taking place the following week. There I found a spiritual teacher to guide me.

Jim Fletcher's thick Dallas drawl was not what I imagined my spiritual teacher would sound like. He invited me to his home for a private session. As he greeted me at his door, he told me of his travels around the world and that he had collected a "few" pieces of art. His home was so crammed with deity statues I walked sideways, my hands tightly gripping my legs, in fear I might knock into one of them tipping them off their pedestals. The size of Jim's collection confirmed the phrase "Everything IS bigger in Texas."

Jim introduced me to the Diamond Heart Approach[36] and he was my teacher for several years. The approach taught about the qualities of Essence.[37] The first lesson was learning the personality types of the Enneagram[38] that block our essential nature. The Diamond Heart practice taught me to see and own the depths of my caretaker personality traits.

I am an Enneagram # 2—the giver or helper. The #2 personality type exalts to the artist and digresses to the boss. It was very painful to see the hooks I had developed to get what I needed. As a true caretaker, I'd derived my self-worth by putting others first and I'd neglected the needs of my inner child. I'd sacrificed myself to gain affection. These were the hooks I'd created with others to survive. At first, it was hard to own this pattern. As a

---

[36] *Diamond Heart Approach:* A spiritual path developed by A.H. Almaas, integrating elements of psychology and spirituality to promote personal transformation and self-realization.

[37] *Essence:* A concept explored in the *Diamond Heart* series of teachings by A.H. Almaas, which emphasizes the inherent qualities of the human soul or "essence." This work delves into the nature of existence, aiming to help individuals recognize and cultivate their true selves beyond egoic structures. Through a blend of spiritual inquiry and psychological insight, the teachings focus on experiencing qualities such as love, strength, and wisdom as essential aspects of personal development and spiritual awakening.

[38] The *Enneagram* is a personality typology describing nine distinct but interconnected patterns of thought, emotion, and behavior, often used in psychology and spiritual practice. See Don Richard Riso and Russ Hudson, *The Wisdom of the Enneagram* (New York: Bantam Books, 1999).

caretaker, I could hold space for others but not for myself. I was neglecting my inner child.

Meeting my Inner Child

I first connected with my inner child in my next session with Jim. My little boy was emaciated, starving, curled up in a ball, and angry from the many years I had neglected him. At first, he wanted nothing to do with me. He didn't trust me, and I didn't know how to care for him. Jim guided me to hold him, and at first, my inner child remained curled and sat motionless. Gradually, he allowed me to hold him as I held my heart. I repeated, "I love you." It took many failed attempts to reconnect with him and develop enough trust to ask what he needed. When I did, he was enraged at me for spending most of my life taking care of other people's needs instead of my needs—and his. I needed to help him release his deep-seated rage.

Caretakers carry an immense amount of rage. So, in our next session, I kicked and screamed and hit pillows, pounding them until my hands and feet throbbed. I felt raw and primal. As I let go of layers of anger, my physical body softened, and my emotional body and inner child felt soothed. I sensed a spaciousness where there had been pain.

A new awareness arose from the space deep inside me. My anger had transformed into a vital essence of strength. I learned how emotions like anger were actually blocked aspects of our essential selves. As I saw how my anger was blocking my strength, a profound sense of protection washed over me.

Super Ego

As I shared this realization with Jim, he began to teach me how I not only needed to love my inner child; I needed to protect him. Jim explained that the *Super Ego* was a part of our personality who absorbed all of the criticism from our parents, teachers, and society at large. The Super Ego was the harsh critical voice within who judged pretty much everything we did, especially the desires of our child.

Being a Virgo sun and a #2 enneagram type, I knew inner criticism all too well. That voice beat me down, like when Dad called me "Big Time." So, over the next few sessions, I practiced reparenting my inner child as a loving parent. I replaced negative self-talk with positive affirmations and encouragement and began the long process of celebrating my strengths and accomplishments. The latter was the most difficult for me.

All of the hooks I had developed in my relationships to get what I needed stemmed from my childhood views of what I needed to do in order to survive and receive love. Owning these aspects of ourselves is a process of understanding the personality and moving toward living a soul-guided life. My studies in the Diamond Heart approach with Jim were teaching me to retrieve my Essence—my soul.

Jim moved to Denver, and most of our men's group lived in Denver. I had lost my spiritual support in Boulder. As beautiful as Boulder was, most everyone was white, except for Tom. I longed for the diversity, opportunities, and vibes a bigger city offers. I opened an office in Denver with four gay health practitioners and was named the best psychotherapist in the Colorado gay newspaper, *Outfront*. The commute was stressful, and I felt a pull to the big city again. When one of the members of our group told me an apartment was available in his building, I knew it was a sign to move.

My time in Boulder was bittersweet. It instilled the importance of being in the present moment, enhanced my skills in somatic therapy, and exposed my shadow wound. As I connected more with my body, I noticed the imbalances; the tension, the pain, the uncomfortable feelings—the very experiences I had been trying to resist. As I deepened my understanding of somatic practices as a student—and later as a budding therapist—I learned to manage and comfort the shame my inner child felt, but it lingered. I could shift my mindset and express my feelings with somatic practices, but until I could hold my inner child and give him the safety he needed to thrive, I repeated patterns and attracted situations that played the same scenarios over again.

Everything repeats itself until it is seen, loved, and no longer needs your attention. Every painful feeling is longing to be seen and loved. So, I had to love my most unlovable parts. As my heart opened to love and my inner child, I began retrieving my soul.

It was the turn of the 21st century. A new trajectory in a new city. It would be a time of solitude and inner searching. I had many questions to answer. *What parts of myself do I still not love? What do I want to do in life? Will I ever be truly successful? Will I ever fall in love again?* The truck was packed, and Harry and I didn't know what was ahead.

"When we feel safe enough to expose our shadows,
that's when we become free."
—Gabby Bernstein

4

The Call to Return Home

Harry cried throughout the thirty-minute drive down I-25 to Denver. As soon as we got inside our new home and he spotted the windows, however, he purred and rolled on the floor as if he had been living there his whole life. Our new apartment was much bigger and in a beautiful old building, a block from Cheeseman Park. There were windows in every room with ledges for Harry to perch on. Being on the first floor, Harry could see the tree-lined street, the squirrels, and all of the activity of city life. He greeted every person who passed by, and they loved talking to him.

I soon took a part-time job at a nearby Whole Foods to supplement my income. The somatic psychology field wasn't widely recognized, so as a young therapist, I struggled to support myself. My spiritual teacher, Jim, sensed my struggle and began planting seeds about a job at a condominium complex where he was the Board president. It would support me financially but meant letting go of my identity as a therapist. I didn't want to let go.

I said no several times before reluctantly accepting the job. As the director of operations and services of a luxury condominium complex in Denver, I took care of some of the world's wealthiest people. I not only ran the operations of the building and managed the budget, vendors, and grounds; I also provided special services. I collected residents' mail when they traveled, watered plants, delivered packages and flowers, and charged their cars in the winter when they lived in their Palm Springs homes. Many of them were incredibly generous to me with gifts and tips, but many had unrealistic expectations of me.

They thought I should fulfill their requests instantly, even though I had no real capability to achieve that. For instance, they threw fits when the elevator broke down, expecting the issue to resolve instantly even when it required ordering and waiting for a new part. They demanded the building to be entirely secure, despite it not being designed for complete sealing.

Despite the challenges, I did learn a lot. I managed a million-dollar budget, coordinating major projects and overseeing countless vendors. Each project turned out better than anticipated and under budget. I became tough—a quality I wouldn't have developed as a therapist. I could easily detect if someone was lying. Most didn't because I met them as equals—I asked about their families and gave them gifts of appreciation. Vendors loved working for me, and because of the respect I gave them, they would bend over backwards to help me.

Nancy was my garden vendor, and we became close friends. Nancy had an intimate relationship with flowers—a reverent dedication. I learned from her that flowers were living beings to not only water but to develop relationships with. Nancy's artistic vision was otherworldly and magical to me. I marveled at Nancy's talents. Her floral creations were overflowing, packed with shapes, sizes, and colors I had never seen. They were works of art. My solace during this job was my time each day in the garden— taking care of these beautiful creations and nurturing this interconnection with the plants I was learning to feel.

Still, I was doing the jobs of three people, and since the Board kept giving me raises, I kept working too hard.

The position offered me financial stability, and I began to relax. Jim and I had sessions every week. We dove deeper into the Diamond Heart Approach. As I continued to protect and re-parent my inner child, my sense of safety increased. Developing the capacity to be comfortable with uncomfortable feelings and overwhelming thoughts increased my consciousness of their origin, and my life shifted. I quit smoking, realizing that what I really wanted was to take a deep breath. With that realization, quitting was incredibly easy.

Embracing this coherence, I began to love myself and feel a greater sense of integrity. I no longer felt the need to conceal myself. The gift of integrating all of the wisdom I received and walking my talk gave me confidence in myself. Then Jim moved to Mexico, and I lost my spiritual support again.

I poured all of my energy into my job, allowing me to purchase a condominium, drive an Acura, and wear high-end Nordstrom clothing. From the outside, my life appeared perfect. I thought I'd attained the American dream.

But in doing so, I neglected my emotional wellbeing, I turned away from many aspects of my spiritual journey and felt disheartened.

American dancer and musician Gabrielle Roth reminds us what a shaman might say to someone expressing disillusionment with their life.[39]

When did you stop dancing?
When did you stop singing?
When did you stop being enchanted by stories?
When did you stop being comforted by the sweet territory of silence?
—Gabrielle Roth

My heart was aching because I had stopped dancing, singing, and sharing my story. I drank myself to sleep to quiet the needy voices in my head. Carrying too much responsibility for one person, I worked overtime everyday and developed chronic insomnia. I had lost my connection to the sacred and felt very alone. Far away from my family and often too busy to visit, I had missed special times with them.

---

[39] Gabrielle Roth, *Maps to Ecstasy: A Healing Journey for the Untamed Spirit* (Novato, CA: New World Library, 1998), 3.

Harry Ignited the Magic

It was April 2013 when I returned to my parents' home to help transport Dad after a triple bypass surgery and a difficult rehabilitation. He experienced a stroke during the surgery and was bound to a wheelchair for the rest of his life. In addition, as predicted by his doctor, Dad's cognitive decline had progressed to Alzheimer's disease. This was the beginning of the very painful experience of his dying. A couple of years before he passed, I began having very strange physical experiences in which I could not control the movements of my body. Some would say I was possessed; some would determine that I had circulation issues. I felt like a puppet—like someone or something was moving me. It was terrifying. Foolishly, I drove myself home from my job both times this occurred and after an hour or so, with Harry resting on my stomach, the sensations would pass.

For the next few years, Dad was not his deep, humorous, immensely creative self. I missed that part of him that was always putting on a show. He'd become angry most of the time, and it reminded me so much of the side of him in which his mean comment, "Who do you think you are, 'Big Time'?" lived.

He wasn't the same man who was madly in love with Mom. Now she had the arduous tasks of feeding, clothing, bathing, pushing his wheelchair, taking him to and from the bathroom, and all the assisted transfers that were required. She loved him so much she began sacrificing her body and life in the name of love. After getting him settled and helping my mother figure out how to take care of him, I returned to Denver to be with my cat, Harry, who was also dying. Harry and I had lived together for almost twenty years, and I didn't want to let go. I was fighting to keep him alive as he gazed at me with vacant eyes.

I reached out to an animal communicator. She sensed he was ready and guided me to hold acupressure points on him, comforting him as we drove to the vet. My tears emanated from the core of my stomach, and my body shook. I had never cried so deeply.

The vet invited me to tell Harry how much I loved him and thank him for everything he gave me and to expect a smell or sensation as his way of communicating back to me. I felt a swoosh of energy as his spirit left his body. As I handed his limp body to the doctor, I paused, searching for a sign from Harry. I couldn't sense anything and became disheartened, especially given how well we knew each other. As I collected my things to leave, I reached for my cell phone, and there was a text from a landline from my work, which wasn't possible. It was in broken prose.. *"I can get the rest of the more comfortable of you are ready to go back to home okay, I just wanna going tonight. I just.. I just wanted...."*

I stood frozen in disbelief. *How was that possible? My cat Harry just sent me a text?* Harry gave me such a blessing! As this experience unfolded, I realized how miraculous it was, especially compared to what I could perceive before that moment. It expanded my awareness of what is possible.

Loss and Solitude

Returning to my empty condo, I was completely distraught and very lonely. I spent over a year grieving. The Native Americans say grieving takes a full year, as each season holds memories. Believing I could never find a sweeter companion, I gave up hope of finding a cat who could replace his special love.

So, I took advantage of living alone to completely gut my condo and remodel. It took over a year to transform a 1980s buildout, in my 1920s building, into a modern 2014 condo with gorgeous, beveled windows. It was open, each room a different shade of purple and blue, my favorite colors. I created a home that became my peaceful sanctuary, and those who visited said they felt the peace. A few months after its completion, I wanted someone to share it with. I had a strong sense, almost a voice, telling me I had to go to the cat shelter very soon.

A few days later, my friend Nicol and her daughter Kendall offered to accompany me. We sat in a room of a hundred cats, running around, sleeping, and hissing at each other. Several cats approached me, but I wasn't sure. I turned my head, and through all of the chaos there was this one white cat lying in a bed cleaning herself, oblivious to the chaos. She had the most beautiful blue eyes I had ever seen. A couple of seconds later, she was by my side, brushing up against my leg, and jumped onto my lap.

Nicol and Kendall, eyes wide, said "Pick her! She's beautiful! You should name her after a queen!"

I said, "Well, two of my nieces are Elizabeth and Kathryn, so…" Then, "Greta" spilled out of my mouth.

It took a couple of days for the paperwork to process. The day I brought her home, my friend Annette came over to meet her, and Greta laid her head on my wrist. That would become her favorite resting place. She had picked me.

A few days later, I got the news that Dad was being placed in hospice care. They estimated he had a couple of months left, prompting me to start planning my return trip. However, the predictions grew increasingly grim; two weeks turned into one week, and then, the morning after my birthday, as I was en route to the airport, I received the heartbreaking call that he had passed away. Tears streaming down my cheeks, the reality that I would never see him again became concrete.

I spent two weeks supporting Mom, making arrangements and planning his service with Uncle Everett. Dad had told me he wanted "Adagio for Strings" by Samuel Barber[40] played at his service. So, I made

---

[40] *Adagio for Strings* is a composition by American composer Samuel Barber, originally arranged in 1938 from the second movement of his String Quartet, Op. 11; it has since

sure it was, not realizing at the time I was the only one he told. With my nephew Matthew, the tech genius, we created a music and video experience. I had his life and songs in my head. It was my tribute to Dad— an otherworldly man, ahead of his time, who touched so many lives but never thought he did enough.

When I returned to Denver after his funeral, I had another weird neurological attack at work. I stumbled to my car, barely making it to my acupuncturist. As I wobbled to her office, my body slammed up against each building. She had this amazing machine called the Avatar that had helped me heal the vertigo I had been experiencing since graduate school.

When we used the Avatar that day, the movement of the graph was erratic, squiggly, and made an eerie sound. *What is going on inside of me? Will I be able to heal this? Am I going crazy?* With the help of my acupuncturist and a medical intuitive, I discovered I was dealing with more than just physical ailments—there was a heavy energetic burden that had been weighing me down for years—and modern medicine couldn't help me. It was beyond the reality most of us accepted. There was an undeniable connection to my father—a mystery waiting to be discovered. The Avatar readings helped set me on a path to confront and release the pressure that had been holding me back, leading me to the transformative experience of Kambo.

Kambo is the name of the secretion of a tropical giant leaf frog from the Amazonian Forest, and it has been used for centuries by local tribes to enhance their hunting skills. At the end of the last century, Kambo was introduced in Europe and the USA as a "healing" intervention to cleanse

---

become one of the most frequently performed American orchestral works. See Barbara B. Heyman, *Samuel Barber: The Composer and His Music* (New York: Oxford University Press, 1992), 205–210.

bodily systems and is regarded as a "detox" intervention. Proponents believe Kambo can purify the physical body of toxic substances, as well as purify the mind and spirit of negative energy.

From Managing to Healing Ancestral Wounds

I found a wonderful healer named Raven Rose, an herbalist and Kambo practitioner. She explained the process, and with her recommendation, I enrolled in a series of ceremonies. During the Kambo ceremonies, she burned small holes into my shoulder with a stick of incense. The venom entered my body when Raven placed the Kambo on these burns. After a few minutes, I felt an intense rush of heat rise through my body. I felt very nauseous and soon was throwing up. During the initial four sessions, I released mucus, which Raven said were emotional-level toxins. During each ceremony there was a deeper layer of release, and I realized I was letting go of the fear of being myself, which, I discovered, I held mostly in my belly.

The last ceremony of five was the most potent. A fiery heat rose from my sacrum. I made it to the bathroom just in time. Splashing cold water on my face, I glanced in the mirror at my pale face. I looked like I was dying. Upon returning to the room and Raven's gentle guidance, I sensed a large, dark, and cloudy energy hovering behind me. The mucus I'd been releasing had turned to bile; it burned with bitterness. This felt bigger than me—like an accumulation of lifetimes of repression. After the venom ran its course, the dark energy dissolved. My death transformed into my rebirth, and I felt an unfamiliar lightness—a sense of freedom I hadn't realized was possible. The heavy burden had been lifted. The dark entity that made sure I stayed small was gone. I no longer heard my father's judgmental voice—I could hear my own voice without the echoes of ancestral judgment.

I curled up in a ball and sipped a soothing mint tea as I integrated what had just happened. I realized that the heavy energy that had left my body was not just my father's. It had been passed along from generations of relatives who were full of self-judgment. Generational ancestral energy had attached to my wound (or maybe it was there the whole time from other lives). I learned that pain travels through families, cultures, and civilizations until someone is ready to feel it and heal it. For many of us, it can feel like a generational curse. Many people bury pain like it didn't happen, but pain demands to be felt. You can't heal pain that you refuse to feel. You have to experience it and then release it.

A deep sense of calm took over my body, and I felt strong, confident, and blissful. My true self emerged in a bigger way. I knew this was not only a personal healing. I'd experienced ancestral healing as well.

After this life-altering experience, I drove home, gently walked up the stairs to my condo, and Greta greeted me as usual. I collapsed on my couch, and she curled up between my legs. I closed my eyes, and the thought of returning to my corporate job became unbearable. Their demands on me rattled my nervous system. I was exhausted and could no longer tolerate the narcissistic behavior of my wealthy clients.

Releasing "Big Time" opened my heart and freed me from playing small. As I took some deep breaths, my mind quieted. In the silence, I knew it was time to follow my heart again. It was then that the idea of creating a healing paradigm I came to call Depth Integration flowed into my awareness.

The Vision of My Mission

I started developing Depth Integration by amalgamating my wellness practices and life experiences, weaving them into a cohesive whole. My spiritual work with Diamond Heart had instilled an emphasis on the soul. Psychotherapy took me far, somatic work took me further, but I wanted to work spiritually with people this time. The question was: *How?*

My dear friend Dee, a playwright who had attended both Stephens and Naropa, helped me draft the opening phrases for my website.

Throughout time all cultures have practiced therapeutic traditions to quiet the mind, reclaim lost aspects of self, and move toward a vitality that is our birthright as human beings on this planet. Depth Integration is the blend of ancient practices with modern healing techniques that supports an intuitive journey using the breath, the body, and a vision of vibrant health and wholeness

As I set up my website and led a couple of shamanic journey workshops in Denver, COVID-19 hit and stopped me in my tracks. *How am I going to continue with my work?* I felt uncertain about my next steps. I believed my work needed to be conducted in person because of its physical nature. Having lost contact with the therapy world for over twenty years, I found it had transformed—no more putting business cards on the bulletin board at Whole Foods! Now, everyone was using the internet. The blessing of COVID was I had to work from home for several months, so I had some time to explore.

With a little research, I discovered that since the essence of my work was energetic, I could facilitate sessions with my clients on the cloud-based video communications platform, Zoom. To familiarize myself with the new digital world, I took part in a coaching cohort in which the leader recommended I enroll in a program focused on hosting a few online summits to expand my audience. My first online summit, *Healing Trauma Through Conscious Embodiment* was very successful. I was surprised with the experts in their fields that I interviewed who said yes to my invitation to present.

After the summit, I sent a questionnaire to all of the participants. The final question was: "If you could sit me down and ask me a question, what would it be?" While reading the responses one day, I couldn't believe one of them: "Are you single?" It took me a few weeks to muster the courage to respond: "Yes."

Daniel checked all the boxes: stunningly handsome, immensely talented in music, brilliant (he spoke five languages) and, to top it off, he was spiritual. We chatted every single night. When I surprised him with a birthday bouquet delivery, he was absolutely floored!

As our connection deepened, my job became stressful. The Board was experiencing financial issues that I had warned them to be prepared for every year I was there. They chose to keep their monthly assessment low and didn't save enough. With new leadership, they began to blame me for their situation. I sensed this was the time to leave. I had some savings and income from the summit, so I took the risk and resigned.

I headed off to Toronto to meet Daniel in person, the day after my final day at the condo complex. He picked me up at the airport, and we both nervously began the conversations one has when acquainted. Daniel was taller and thinner than he looked on Zoom, but just as handsome. As he opened the door to his condo, I thought I had walked into a dream. His brilliant all-white condo was a museum of vibrant colored paintings, sculptures, and antiques, each artistically placed—calling my attention. Floor-to-ceiling windows opened to a view of the Toronto skyline— straight out of a movie. Ten stairs led to his loft bedroom. I hadn't slept with a man in thirty years and felt shy. Each night before bed, we listened to an old Louise Hay meditation of his as we held hands.

The long weekend was magical. We had so much in common—our love of theater, opera, and symphony. Tony played his accordion, and I savored his tiramisu—a special family recipe. We both lit up, belting out show tunes while he tickled the ivories, until his neighbor rang up with a polite request for a little quiet.

Cuddled up on the couch, we spent much of the weekend laughing together while solving crossword puzzles. Daniel began experiencing a painful lower-back problem that often forced him to lie flat on his back. This issue arose after we started our relationship, and as a therapist, I couldn't help but connect the timing to our bond. I gave him a psoas massage, which really gave him relief until it was time for me to return to Denver.

I found myself in tears at the airport; my heart felt so open after such a long time without being in a relationship.

When I landed back in Denver, I juggled producing my second *Healing Trauma through Conscious Embodiment* summit with our nightly calls, nursing Greta (she had developed kidney disease), and joining a new coaching program.

My second summit was special because Katie Hendricks was one of the presenters. Interviewing her, I revisited my roots in Conscious Embodiment—the Hendricks Method. My foundation was summoned through this connection from my past.

My summits and new coaching program fostered new connections with some of the presenters, who guided me to aspects of myself I had not explored yet, shifting my trajectory. Three women, Monique, DaeEss 1Drea, and Connie became phenomenal influences on my spiritual journey.

Monique Lang, from my first summit, felt like an old friend. There was an ease in our connection that felt ancient. Her gracious heart connected me to many wonderful people who presented at my summits. She told me she took people on sacred journeys to Ecuador, and I felt guided to go on her next adventure in August, a couple of months away.

Meanwhile, the stress of caregiving for Greta wore on me. Kidney disease is a roller coaster of highs and lows. She received monthly fluids and steroid injections and afterwards Greta was a kitten again—jumping heights that seemed impossible, devouring her food, and making me laugh, dashing through the house suddenly for no apparent reason. Toward the end of each month, she slowly spiraled into lethargy—not eating and losing more weight; she got down to six pounds.

Daniel had recently lost his dog, so he knew what I was feeling. During our nightly calls, his empathy and compassion meant so much to me. Daniel loved my performance as a coach, born of our love for theater. He attended some of my online classes and was the first to like my posts. I felt supported by his actions and began to share what I desired in a relationship and how commitments were essential to creating the safety for authentic sharing, which supports each person's highest potential. I shared two commitments from the Hendricks' *Conscious Loving* book.[41]

"I commit to acting from the awareness that I am 100% the source of my reality.

I commit to revealing myself fully in my relationships, not to concealing myself."

When I uttered the word "commitment," it was met with silence. This time, it wasn't "I don't think I can do that" like Tom said, but the silence wasn't a "Yes, let's do that." I was determined to show my vulnerability in our relationship. My desire would be met with fixing instead of acceptance.

Through it all, Greta was a devoted teacher of unconditional love, and she was, as her sister Auntie Lea, called her, "my little angel." Her support helped me juggle everything on my plate.

The last ball I was juggling was my new spiritual wealth coaching program with Corrina Steward. I desired to create my business based

---

[41] Gay Hendricks and Kathlyn Hendricks, *Conscious Loving: The Journey to Co-Commitment* (New York: Bantam Books, 1990), xx.

on spiritual principles. Corrina was a guest teacher in my first coaching program that taught me to produce summits, and I felt guided to learn from her. She taught me money is energy, and through her activations,[42] we travelled to different dimensions to receive guidance and support on how to not only create abundance but to "Be" the energy of abundance.

One of the support coaches in the program was Connie Weilke, a Reiki Master. I scheduled a private session with her, and it was far from any Reiki session I had experienced. As Connie began our session, she opened the portal—I didn't know what a portal was. She created a golden spiral to protect me and Greta and told all of the spirits that were not of Divine light to leave. "NOW," she emphasized. She told me Greta was not a cat, which I knew, and what "they" were telling her. I wasn't sure who "they" were, but I would find out soon.

During our program, Corrina shared an opportunity to write a chapter in a book one of her friends, Paula Jessup, was publishing. I contacted Paula, met with her friend Brian Benson, and proceeded to write my chapter—the first I had ever written for a book. Paula and Brian helped me every step of the process. In their book *Dare to Dream*, my chapter "Who Do You Think You Are?" addressed the childhood trauma I'd overcome while creating Depth Integration.

As I finished juggling these balls, it was time to visit Daniel again. It was the end of July, and on this trip, I saw another side of him. It started out where we left off. We took a day trip to Toronto Island via the ferry. Walking around the island, holding hands, we dreamed about living in one of the quaint cottages and talked to a peacock at the children's zoo. It was an extremely hot and humid summer day, and we had walked several miles both to and from the dock.

---

[42] *Spiritual Activations* are practices or energetic transmissions believed to awaken latent spiritual capacities, raise consciousness, or catalyze transformation in the practitioner. See William Bloom, *The Power of Modern Spirituality: How to Live a Life of Compassion and Personal Fulfilment* (London: Piatkus, 2011).

Returning back to his condo, exhausted and dehydrated, I desperately needed a shower. Daniel had a gorgeous, white tiled master bathroom with a chain curtain for show, not for function, and a drain without a slope. It was how many gays designed our homes, more for the "wow" effect, less for the practical. There was a method to drain the water that pooled during the shower with a squeegee mop. The rug under the sinks, beside the shower, had to be rolled up and then replaced after squeegeeing. I was shown how to do this on my first trip.

His bathroom was an addition, elevated above the main floor by two sturdy wooden steps. After completing my task, I slipped into some shorts and as I stepped out the doorway, my feet lost traction, sending me airborne. I landed heavily on the hard wooden steps with a loud thud. Daniel exclaimed, "Why didn't you wipe your feet?!" in an irritated tone that I struggled to understand. He continued, "I'm glad you checked your insurance before you came..."

I stood frozen, overwhelmed by shock and intense pain. Dark bruises began to form on my arms and lower back, the areas that had taken the brunt of my fall. I thought to myself, No "Are you okay?" and then, I shut down. My shock felt like when Dad would suddenly blame me for not doing something correctly, without showing me how to do it.

This wasn't the man I had been talking to for six months. There was an incongruence. On the phone he spoke poetically of spiritual ideals, choosing love over fear, and his words pulled me in.

But each time I'd tried to be intimate with Daniel, something held me back. Taking full responsibility for my feelings, I questioned whether I was afraid of intimacy, but I sensed something deeper at play. My upset stomach gurgled, my nervous system felt unsafe, and I struggled to sleep in his presence. Too eager to make this connection work, I abandoned my soul, overlooking the wisdom my body was trying to convey. Pretending I was happy, I didn't stand in my power of authenticity—my sovereignty. I was not coherent.

Over the next few days, Daniel introduced me to his best friends and sister. Each one pulled me aside and asked me when I was moving to Toronto. My response was "that is up to Daniel." Their excitement fueled my belief that Daniel and I were meant to be together, and yet I still wasn't sure.

As we continued to become acquainted, I learned Daniel's former partner of twenty years was Ecuadorian. I was surprised to hear he didn't talk to his mother about his sexuality and when they'd had dinner with her, he was a "friend."

Despite these challenges, our souls loved each other. As he shared memories of his past visits to Ecuador, the visions began fueling the anticipation for my upcoming trip. The morning of my flight back to Denver, I placed several love notes under his bed—my friend Nancy had inspired me to create them—one for each day of my trip. As we drove to the airport, Daniel voiced his fear that I might not want to be in a relationship upon my return. *"Why would he say that?"* I wondered.

"You build inner strength through embracing the totality of your experience, both the delightful parts and the difficult parts."
— Pema Chödrön

5

My First Sacred Journey

Why would he say that? I wondered during my flight back to Denver. When I landed, I only had a week to pack for my trip. I took Lea out to dinner, mostly to thank her for spending so much time taking care of Greta. Lea is one of the most compassionate listeners I know. She wears her heart on her sleeve, but when something bothers her, she becomes a warrioress. While sharing about my trip, she said of Daniel's reaction after my fall, "That's not right!" Her words stayed in the back of my mind as I packed.

As I boarded my flight to Quito, Ecuador, I wondered what my sacred journey had in store for me. I felt that I was missing a skill as a healer and wanted to discover what that was. That was my intention for this expedition to the equator.

I heard that Grandmother, what the indigenous people of South America call the plant medicine Ayahuasca,[43] didn't give you what you wanted. Instead, she always gave you what you needed. I discovered the truth of that statement in ways that I still don't completely understand or have words for.

---

[43] *Ayahuasca:* A psychoactive brew made from Amazonian plants, traditionally used in ceremonial contexts by Indigenous tribes for spiritual healing and exploration of consciousness.

I arrived in the gorgeous country of Ecuador at midnight, and a sweet young woman with the piercings and tattoos of her generation was waiting for me at the airport with a sign. She was the daughter of my host shaman and giggled through her braces, graciously welcoming me, as we drove to my hotel in the dark.

After a short sleep, I was greeted by the innkeeper Patricia, a kind woman whose soft smile made me feel at home. My journey mates slowly shuffled into the breakfast room. The glass-enclosed room had stunning views of the lush green tropical mountains, as tall but softer than the Rocky Mountains I saw every day in Colorado. After a breakfast of avocados, tropical fruit I had never seen, and traditional scrambled eggs, the taxis arrived to drive us to what would be our home base for the next four days. This homestead consisted of a white stone house, a sweat lodge, a fire pit, and the bamboo house. The grounds were decorated with numerous tall clumps of San Pedro cacti stalks, old sacred canopy trees, who later spoke to me, and a vibrant array of flowering medicinal plants—tropical oranges, yellows, reds, and blues.

Ecuador felt like more than a destination. It was a return to the roots of something timeless and sacred. It reminded me that healing is not just a personal act—it is a reconnection to the wisdom of the earth and the ancestors who walk with us. Everyone is family. The shamans greeted me as if we had met before. They were connecting to my ancient soul. I met Monique in person for the first time and was surprised by her tiny body— her soul has a powerful presence. She wore a traditional white Ecuadorian dress with a colorful embroidered neck and sleeves. Her blue eyes glistened as she said, "Welcome to Ecuador."

The first two days I met each shaman individually, receiving blessings, insights, healings, and encouragement. As I approached the fire pit for my first session, I sensed the peaceful, yet powerful, energy of the man standing by the fire. My sense of time slowed down as I entered the sacred space he created. Shairy, dressed in all white with a colorful headband accentuating his flowing long black hair, nodded in reverence as he reached out his hands to greet me. His gentle gaze had a depth of wisdom I had only sensed with the Dali Llama. As he motioned for me to take a seat in the wood chair next to him, he said, "Your color is purple." Purple is my favorite.

Shairy went on to say, "You need to own your gifts and be grateful to the spirits for them." I didn't have to tell him I never allowed myself to embrace the power of my gifts. Shairy was a sound healer and bent over to pick the exact flute from the array of his collection laying on a blanket to his left. As I closed my eyes to absorb the soothing timbre, he said, "I see a light shining down upon your head from the hole in the roof." You possess the energy of the jaguar. You will guide others through their darkness, helping them confront their fears and connect with their inner power."

I learned the jaguar is a master over both the physical and spiritual realms—sensing beyond the surface, integrating the dark and light parts. The jaguar delves into the shadow self to reclaim personal power by turning fear to strength. At the end of our session, he gave me a purple candle to take back to my room. Shairy said, "This purple candle is your power. Light it before you sleep and give your fears to the flame."

Trust, Surrender, Joy, and Lightness

My next private healing session was my first meeting with Tati, our Ecuadorian host. Her eyes glowed with ancient wisdom. Tati is a very strong soul with a humble voice. Carrying a bright colored pouch, she guided down a hill to an ancient tree that we sat under for our session.

Her precise movements honored the territory (what she calls the land). I watched as she checked how the wind was blowing; she noticed every nuance. Tati was in relationship with all of the spirits of the earth, and she listened intensely and allowed them to guide her.

We sat on a grass mat under the tree, and Tati burned some sage to cleanse us. She reached into her pouch and pulled out a metal pipe and a small round box. Inside was a special tobacco powder—rapeh.[44] She poured a small amount in her palm and scooped half of the powder into the short end of the pipe. Tati touched my heart with one hand and made a cross in the air followed by a circle with the pipe with the other. She inserted the pipe into my left nostril and blew forcefully.

My head exploded and tears welled in my eyes as she said, "Breathe softly through your mouth." Tati repeated the process in my right nostril. After the initial shock, the rapeh rapidly dropped me into present-moment awareness.

As I continued to breathe, she asked, "Gregg, what direction do you feel called to?"

I said, "I guess 'Oeste' or West, since my last name is Westwood."

As we turned to face the West, a hummingbird appeared and paused, motionless for what seemed like a full minute. From this miraculous creature's qualities, Tati uncovered the message with me. She asked me to name four qualities (for the four directions) I received from the hummingbird. "Okay, so place each one with a direction—first in front of you, then to your back, and then your left and right." To my front was Trust, to my back was Surrender, to my left was Joy, and to my right was Lightness. To this day, this is my mantra.

[44] *Rapé* (also spelled *rapeh*) is a sacred Amazonian snuff made from powdered tobacco and medicinal plants, traditionally used in shamanic ceremonies for grounding, cleansing, and prayer. See Michael J. Winkelman, "Traditional Use of Amazonian Psychoactive Plant Preparations in Shamanism and Religion," in *Psychoactive Plants and Society*, ed. Michael J. Winkelman and Thomas B. Roberts (Westport, CT: Greenwood Press, 2007), 35–76.

After having private healing sessions with several shamans the first day, the group of eight who joined me on this journey gathered together the next morning to take part in a therapy called "Family Constellations." I'd been aware of how being a caretaker had weighed on me, but this became even more apparent in my session. I'd never wanted to see anyone in pain, especially people I love, but I realized that diving in to assist anyone who was suffering was a coping mechanism for me as well. To survive, I'd developed my caregiving skills at a very young age.

Releasing the Secret Burden

Family Constellations is a group therapeutic method developed by Bert Hollinger, in which other members of the group represent members of your family and interact based on what they feel in the present moment.

The eight of us joined together for this journey in Ecuador, Monique and Tati leading. Tati lit a cigar of sacred tobacco and puffed it as she circled the group. She seemed to be receiving guidance on where to place people and how to have them move. For me, what occurred was miraculous. Each person who played my family members captured their personalities and pains without ever meeting them. My brother is a man of few words, and the woman playing him said, "I can't speak." This process revealed secret sexual abuse that had occurred in my family, which I had sensed had happened. Since no one else acknowledged it, I thought I was mistaken. Tati said I was carrying the burden.

As I saw how each member related to this family dynamic and felt so much compassion for my family members, it became clear that I was carrying a burden, especially for Mom and Grandma Tommie. Two memories streamed into my consciousness. The first was Mom's reaction when I gave her *The Courage to Heal*. The other was sitting watching an *Oprah* show with Grandma Tommie before she died.

The show's topic was on rape. As we watched women telling their horrific memories, I noticed my grandma's body tense up, and she began fidgeting. Her fists clenched, and then, all of a sudden, she blurted out, "You son of a bitch!" At that moment, I couldn't help but sense something traumatic had happened to her too. Since it was a secret, I didn't trust my thoughts—but my heart knew.

I sat, tears streaming down my cheeks, as Tati handed the person playing me a very heavy rock from the yard. Tati instructed her to pass the rock to my "mother" and "grandmother." They passed it back to the perpetrator, and the perpetrator gave the heavy rock to a person personifying the Universe, who took it out of the bamboo house.

As the symbolic rock left the house, I realized again that all of us bear not only our own pain but that of generations who preceded us. Healing is more than an individual journey—it's a way to honor and release the heavy burdens carried by those who came before us, our ancestors.

For years, I had managed my pain and stress, but now I felt a shift—this was more than just managing. It was a release, a return to a more authentic version of myself. Healing is not changing who you are. It is letting go of who you are not, unbecoming who the world taught you to be. This ritual of handing back my burdens to their origin is one that I now practice often. It reminds me of how interconnected we are and my connection to all creation.

The rest of the shamans were women, which is very uncommon in South American culture. I was so honored to be blessed with so much of the Divine Feminine for my healing experience! They all confirmed that I was a healer and already had my gifts. I just didn't believe in my abilities. They kept saying, "You are ready, Gregorio." They talked of how my role was to hold people's hands as I guided them into their darkness, and after a healing occurred, I would accompany each soul up and into the light of transcendence.

On the fourth day of our journey, we gathered for a ten-hour sweat-lodge ceremony, held in the presence of San Pedro[45] medicine. Local singers joined us, and again, all of the major roles, all the way to the fire keeper, were women. After several rounds of the medicine, served in cups, and heat, we were given rocks to cleanse and bless ourselves with. Mine was a black heart-shaped rock from the Rio Nupe, a headwater of the Amazon River. I felt drawn to rubbing it on my heart, solar plexus, and my lower abdomen and genitals. Since it was pitch black inside, I felt safe massaging the rock on those areas of my body. After the healing was finished, I passed rock, and it was carried out of the lodge to be blessed and released.

When the flaps of the lodge closed to begin the third round, from the pitch black darkness, I heard Tati's voice call out to me, "Gregorio, sing," and someone handed me a rattle. I froze, just like I did as a kindergarten boy. *Who am I to lead a song in this sacred sweat lodge ceremony?* I had never sang with medicine before. Allowing the medicine of San Pedro to hold me, I took a deep breath, found the rhythm of the rattle, and began singing the song of the Eagle that I learned in the sweat lodge in California "Hey neynah heynah" The song surged through me with intensity, reminding me of the way my voice carried confidently on stage and the immense joy and power it once brought me.

I sang four rounds, and during the third round, everyone joined in during the chorus. Their joyful singing sent chills down my spine and throughout my entire Being. I was beaming in disbelief at what had just happened. The sacred medicine had given me the courage to allow Spirit to flow through me. At the time, I did not grasp that I had just led a part of

---

[45] *San Pedro:* a cactus containing the psychoactive substance mescaline, used in traditional healing ceremonies in South America, known for inducing visions and promoting emotional insights.

a sacred ceremony. However, the medicine and Tati's belief in me instilled a strength that would begin to hold on its own.

After spending ten hours in the sweat lodge, every morsel of food and drink was sacred at our dinner. After a deep sleep, we met at our Mercedes mini bus and took to the road for the next few days. Driving by the snow-capped volcanoes of the Andes was breathtaking. Stopping at a colorful market, I picked out my all white native Ecuadorian outfit for the final ceremony in a few days. Then we boarded the bus and were off to the Cloud Forest, a chilly, misty, lush forest with thousands of hummingbirds buzzing by my ear. Beginning at the market and intensifying through the rest of the trip, I was purging from both ends. Some would say that it was food poisoning, but only a couple of us were having this experience. I couldn't help but imagine that Grandmother Ayahuasca was cleansing and preparing me for our time together the following evening. So, I spent most of the time in the cloud forest in my bamboo hut penthouse with the soft drips of the misty rain landing on the windows above my head. I slept like a baby.

On our way back to Quito for the final ceremony, the bus stopped and we picked up a woman with deep brown eyes and soft brown skin, dressed in a long flowing white tunic and pants with a navy blue turban covering her hair. She was the shaman who led the ayahuasca ceremony that evening. Her gentle energy was inviting and spacious.

We spent a few hours in our new hotel, resting for the all-night journey that we were about to embark on. As we boarded the taxis and returned to our original home for the ceremony, I was in a focused state of intention, and my body tingled with anticipation to meet Grandmother. It was the last night of my journey. As I entered the bamboo house, the smoky scents of Palo Santo and sage wafted through the candlelit room, and it glowed with a sacred presence. The shaman and her altar were in the corner in front of me, and there was one empty seat by itself next to the altar. I had to take it.

I approached for my first cup of tea. The shaman handed me the cup with sacred intention, and I drank the medicine with respect for what I was about to experience. I returned to my seat and within a few minutes I saw a kaleidoscope of jaguars intertwined with vivid, bold colors and shapes that were definitely South American. With my intention of growing as a healer, I opened my eyes to witness this healing ceremony.

Then something very heavy descended upon me. My head dropped, and I felt dizzy and nauseous. I reached in front of me for the bucket that was given to each of us at the beginning of the ceremony. I was being called to surrender deeply without any guarantee of where this process was taking me. I knew there was something I needed to let go of to heal myself at the deepest level. This was what this sacred journey was about for me.

As I gazed into the bucket, spirits were coaxing me into a spiral. They told me it was my role to hold people's hands as we dove into the darkness. So I took a deep breath and mustered the courage to surrender and let go completely. It was as though my body dissolved into the space around me.

The act of purging emanated from my sacrum, and the pain was excruciating. It was like each dry heave originated in my pelvis and shot upwards through my throat. But nothing was coming out of me except air. Suddenly, what felt like a little chunk, a physical manifestation of an emotional blockage, dislodged and flew into the plastic bucket.

I collapsed back into the bamboo wall, depleted and weightless. Then I heard this incredible lullaby floating into my energy field. It was like my spiritual mother was holding and rocking me and singing softly into my ears. Her feminine tones and words were angelic, and the soothing melody enveloped every cell of my being. My breathing became soft, and I sunk into her embrace. The shaman sounded like she was singing just for me. *Is that possible?* I wondered.

I heard about this element of the ceremony called *icaros* afterward. The *icaros*—ancient healing songs passed down for generations—felt like a bridge between worlds, carrying me deeper into my healing. Their melodies soothed my inner child and gave my voice the courage to rise with new strength.

In Amazonian tradition, *icaros* are sung by healers during ceremonies to restore balance and release energetic blockages. They may be directed toward the conscious or subconscious mind, the body as a whole, or specific organs. Through these songs or chants, a healer can bring recalibration, love, sensory awakening, emotional release, insight, or whatever else the soul most needs. They are songs of pure light—evoking divine, blissful states while performing profound energetic repair.

It was then that my body became flushed with an incredible amount of warmth and saturated with this enormous glow. Everywhere I looked, there was love. The amount of unconditional love, forgiveness, and joy that I was experiencing was a hundred fold more than I could ever imagine feeling in my body, and it overtook my mind.

Then, just like in the sweat lodge, I heard the voice of the shaman calling on me from the darkness. "Gregorio, sing."

"What?" I said. I froze again. This time I didn't have a song. My Spanish was very limited. *What can I sing that would be meaningful for this sacred ceremony?*

She replied, "Just sing." I closed my eyes and took a deep breath, allowing Grandmother to hold me as I opened my crown chakra and heart and allowed Spirit to flow into my body and fill my heart. As I opened my mouth, tones flowed out of me, creating this angelic, etheric, and soothing melody I couldn't have come up with on my own. This beautiful flow of energy cascading through me touched every soul and spirit in that little bamboo house and beyond. *In that moment, I realized I was no longer just coping—I was healing, allowing light to replace the darkness I had carried for so long.*

As I approached the altar for my last cup of tea, the shaman said that my second chakra opened. The purpose of my sacred journey had been revealed. The medicine helped my purge and let go of the burden of carrying Mom and Grandma Tommie's sexual abuse. The release had opened a channel of energy flow in my body that had been shut down since I was a very young boy. When my second chakra opened, I felt my blood flow into my genitals in a way that I had never experienced before. I had felt ashamed of my sexual energy. At times, it was as if the energy of my genitals felt shriveled. I could never completely figure out why. I thought maybe it was because I was ashamed to be gay. Letting go of the burden not only opened up my sexual energy, but my creative energy, as well. Most importantly, this opened up a much deeper connection with the Divine and a renewed sense of my purpose and gifts as a healer.

My hands began moving, almost like I was a marionette. I used my breath as my hands softly pushed and carved the space in front of me. I was being guided how to move energy. The shaman said that she witnessed light emanating from my hands as I practiced my new craft.

My right hand moved toward my forehead in half of a prayer gesture as the tip of my first finger touched my third eye. This gesture brought me into a focused alignment with the fire. This powerful focus had no distractions, only connection to the Divine in the present moment. This gesture has become a life practice to return me to alignment, focus, and balance.

After the ceremony, the shaman said, "Gregorio, your voice grounded the ceremony. It was needed at that exact time." Again, I was guided and trusted to lead and provide healing for a ceremony that I wasn't at all familiar with. But I was familiar. I had sung those tones before, just not in this lifetime. The shaman later told me that I was a pillar of light for her during the ceremony. *Could this be real?* I was just being myself. I had asked the medicine to show me my healing powers. *Was this my power?*

It takes so much courage to surrender, trust, and let go in the healing process when you often do not know where the process will take you. When we are willing to express and release our feelings fully, on the other side of our pain is always an infinite amount of light, love, forgiveness, joy, and compassion. Trusting and surrendering to sacred medicine can clear wounds that may otherwise take years of therapy to access and heal. It definitely did for me. And I have been on a very deep spiritual healing path since the 1980s.

My sacred journey was discovering that I already have all that I need inside to be a healer. The shamans and the sacred medicine helped me clear away the doubts and blocks to owning my gentle strength, which is my true power. I was born with divine light and gifts. Again, I was trusted to lead and provide healing for a ceremony that I wasn't at all familiar with, yet I was. The purpose of my sacred journey had been revealed. I am not only a healer, but I am a leader. I now intended to own them, be grateful for them, and share them with the world.

When I returned to my hotel room after my first sacred medicine ceremony, my bliss state of unconditional love met a formidable foe. When I closed my eyes, wounded spirits with deformed faces surged, reaching for me in desperation. Unable to sleep, I jumped out of bed and jiggled my body, trying to shake them off. Attempting to muster my strength, I swung my fists and punched the air to fend them off, yet they refused to go away.

I focused on my breath, yet when I closed my eyes, the spirits remained. Overwhelmed and unsure of how to handle their presence, I grasped my heart. With my next breath, I felt an urge to send them love, so I poured heartfelt affection toward them. Almost immediately, their faces softened, transformed, and began to dissolve. The act of radiating my love unconditionally was now integrated into my psyche and soul.

The next morning, I was to return home. While resting under the protective branches of a sacred tree, I spoke with Tati about my experience the night before; of my desire to embody unconditional love and how shaky and vulnerable I felt. She tapped a stunning black condor feather on my head and along my body. The energy I absorbed from this majestic bird grounded me, allowing my nervous system to unwind.

My profound experience of pure, unconditional love was so incredible, I asked myself: *Is it truly possible to embody this state all of the time?*

Before I left, Tati shared a story about a doctor in Argentina who could send the vibration of a plant to patients by calling the energy of the plant. The medicine of the plant would come to the patient; they didn't need to ingest a tincture, just receive the vibration. She said we have just forgotten how to do it. It is so exciting that we are remembering what we had forgotten.

As we hugged goodbye, Tati said, "Remember, Gregorio, the path forward is like the snake. Take your time."

After landing in Denver, I slept for hours and had to walk in slow motion for several days, mindful of each step. Beginning to realize the magnitude of my awakening, I had to honor the pace my body needed to integrate. My friends wanted to hear about my trip.

On my second night home my friend Annette surprised me with an early birthday present—a ticket to the Alicia Keys Concert. Our seats were amazing, just a few rows from the stage, and mine was in the aisle. Alicia left the stage and walked into the audience as she sang "Empire State of Mind." As she approached our row, she took my hand and looked into my eyes. She's incredibly beautiful in person, and her eyes emanated such love from her heart. My senses were so heightened—the bliss I was integrating from Ecuador became embodied in my heart.

The following night, Daniel also surprised me with, "I want to come and visit you for your birthday."

Daniel was allergic to cats, so I scrambled to figure out how his visit would work. My friend Annette was so excited for me; she generously offered her homes to us for the next few days while Lea took care of Greta. First, we stayed at her gorgeous house a block from Denver's most beautiful Washington Park. After spending the night, the next morning we headed up to the High Country. A deer greeted us when we pulled into the driveway of Annette's mountain home in Silverthorne. Daniel and I stayed there for a couple of days, hiking, cooking, and relaxing in the hot tub, star gazing. The stars are so brilliant in the mountains.

On our last night, we said goodbye to the stars and went inside to get ready for bed. As I was about to take a shower, Daniel said, "Make sure you wipe your feet. I don't want you to slip and hurt yourself again." My body stiffened as my eyes flipped back into my skull. I wanted to scream, "The only time I have ever slipped and fell was coming out of *your* bathroom!" I kept my rage inside and shut down, confused. I knew his comment came from a place of care, but it also felt like a backhanded remark. And I knew if I shared my anger, I would be discounted. I tossed and turned all night.

The next morning, we headed to Aspen, driving Independence Pass, which is only open in the summer. Waterfalls cascading into pools, vistas where we could see for miles, and the beautiful Aspen trees lining the highway are always spectacular. Mom treated Daniel and I for two nights in a suite at the stunning St. Regis. As we arrived, the front desk welcomed us with a glass of champagne. The next morning we hiked to the Maroon Bells, and when we returned to the suite, champagne and chocolates were delivered for my birthday.

Mom had treated me to such a lavish birthday. experience. That coupled with Annette's generosity gave us beautiful nesting places; we were treated like royalty. Daniel treated me to my birthday dinner, but it was as though we were treating him to my birthday week.

Waking up the next morning, Daniel was aroused and jumped straight into his urges. I felt like I could have been anyone. A body, not a soul. I had a difficult time connecting and was not aroused. I need foreplay, a slow intimate connection, before I can "perform." He asked me if I wanted to talk, and unfortunately, I said no. I missed the chance to ask for what I needed.

The next morning, we returned to Denver, and Daniel met my friends Lea and Annette. After his visit, they both expressed their concerns. There was a theme that others were seeing that I wasn't willing to. I was giving more than I was receiving, my pattern. Rooted in feeling unworthy to receive, I take full responsibility for that dynamic and yet I longed for a more equal relationship.

Daniel got COVID when he returned to Toronto, and I sent flowers. We talked every night, and it seemed that I was his only support. His friends weren't calling to check in with him, and he felt lonely. I shared my vulnerability about feeling insecure about where my life was heading, and his response was, "Snap out of it." He wasn't willing or able to allow me to share my fear. One of the reasons I didn't ask for what I needed. It didn't seem like I would get it. I didn't feel supported. Even so, I kept trying. He was mirroring my insecurity—still feeling like I should keep it all together.

In October, I returned for what would be my last visit to Toronto. The trip began awkwardly. We were supposed to attend an art show of his dear friend, Carolyn. She and I had a wonderful heartfelt connection, and attending her show was the impetus for my trip. Daniel and I walked several miles to her studio, and it was closed. He had not looked at the invitation. We spent several hours on the bus both ways to and from the event and returned to his condo around midnight.

No "Wow I messed up..." We barely talked, and it would be the theme of this visit. The tension kept building each day. I was writing my chapter in *Dare to Dream*, he was working, and we met for meals.

The next night, I had a Reiki session scheduled with Connie and I asked, "Tony, do you want to join us?"

He said, "Sure."

Connie began, as usual, by commanding all spirits and energies who didn't belong to leave, but one would not. Soon, I learned why.

The night before I left, I expressed I was sad to leave, and Daniel returned with, "Don't think of the negative. Think positive." I felt so dismissed from his statement, I couldn't sleep.

As he drove me to the airport, his last words were, "You should write your own book." It was already in my head.

Upon returning home, I called Daniel, trying one last time to ask for deeper intimacy in our relationship. I was mostly referring to our sharing. I kept pushing for something that wasn't there between us. He replied, "I've checked with my guidance, and I'm not romantically attracted to you. I do love you and I want to be friends." I froze. My spirit shattered. Daniel went on to say, "Don't you?"

I paused and realized that I didn't feel attracted to him, either, even though I kept trying to be. I realized that I had held an image of him and us that was a fantasy. *So, if we can't be intimate with each other now, how can I be friends with him?*

He pleaded for me to continue to find out what our souls were meant to discover together. The words were beautiful, but they didn't land in my body.

I realized some triggers can be moved through quickly. Others take time. His "snap out of it" didn't acknowledge there are layers to healing. Not every trigger can be flipped into a positive in an instant. When I did that, I lost the integrity and depth of my experience. While it was always my intention to remain grateful and positive, bypassing and not fully addressing challenging feelings felt inauthentic to me.

This dynamic in our relationship ended up propelling me further with my intention to love all parts of myself unconditionally, especially my vulnerability. Daniel had simply been mirroring back to me what I could not love in myself. This dynamic wasn't random for me, as I believe that each relationship has lessons I can learn from.

I believe we have soul contracts with others we meet and have relationships with in this lifetime. Many souls we have known in past lives, and that is why they feel so familiar to us. Agreements between our souls with lessons and challenges facilitate our mutual evolution.

As I was in the process of completing my soul contract with Daniel, my desire to move on, I shared my words with Connie for her feedback. I intended to do so with love and appreciation. In our conversation, she revealed additional insights from our session that night in Toronto. Connie mentioned that the other energy present, the one who wouldn't leave, had conveyed to her that it was shielding Daniel from my influence and healing. Although my intention was never to heal him, this disclosure validated my feelings. I realized the energy I sensed in our session with Connie had always been in our relational field.

It had been palpable yet invisible, linked to him, and its presence made me quite uncomfortable.

Certain people enter our lives for a purpose, helping us to open our hearts and trust our instincts. I am so grateful for the love and support Daniel gave to me. Our relationship, though heartbreaking for me, deepened my compassion for myself. It strengthened my intuitive sense and sparked my curiosity, motivating me to explore the intriguing realm of subtle energies. It became an exhilarating journey I was determined to master. The intimacy I was talking about was he wouldn't let me into his world very far, especially his heart. I was crying because he wanted me to stop. My friends saw the dynamic clearly, and I didn't want to.

Feelings of inadequateness rose from our breakup. I met most of them, but the feeling of not being enough took over, and I turned back to scrolling through erotic images for comfort. This time I was conscious, knowing where the desire came from. That is a good first step in breaking an addiction, being conscious. I made the mistake of wishing Daniel a Merry Christmas, and he thought I was connecting again, so I had to end the relationship with more finality—wishing him the best always. I went outside in the snow, burned what I wrote, and buried it.

Fortunately, my behavior didn't last long, but it took another year to move through my grief. While grieving, I spent the next few weeks preparing for and launching my third online summit, *The Conscious Embodiment Summit*, in February. This summit was live over three days. On the last day of my summit, Kimberly stayed on the feed after the last presentation and introduced herself. She said, "I feel called to connect with you."

As our conversation unfolded, so many common threads arose. We both studied at Naropa and were also students of indigenous ways. Immediately we felt called to create something together. Kimberly's joyful smile radiated through her eyes, and I sensed a lightness in her demeanor, a "hang loose" energy, fostered from living in Kauai for many years. She was attending a retreat, with one of the summit's presenters, in Africa in a few weeks, and I was returning to Ecuador in March, so we agreed to connect once we returned to the U.S.

Dare to Dream was launching the week after my summit. I had been healing so much from my Ayahuasca ceremony, I was eager to immerse myself in more healing and inner revelation. So I was returning to Ecuador in March.

Puerto Rican Portals

Before my second journey to Ecuador, I was going to meet my coaching class for Master Mind in Puerto Rico. The weekend before, Nancy invited me to a brunch. We had a lot to catch up on, and I shared about writing this book and my upcoming trips. Over the past few months, she had been struggling with not knowing her true life's path. I would ask her about her struggles, and she would say, "Let's talk about you." That was our pattern. Naively, that is what I was doing—talking only about myself. After several glasses of champagne, out of nowhere, Nancy blurted out, "You are like all my Virgo friends, self-centered! You didn't even notice the Band-Aid on my finger. I cut part of my finger while cooking! It's all about you!" She was seething. Initially, I froze. Her outburst caught me off guard and reminded me of the shock I often felt with Dad. This was not a new dynamic in our connection, and it stoked my feeling of walking on eggshells with her.

Determined to stay present and accountable, I took a deep breath, intending to honor her feelings and share my perspective. I said, "I don't think I am like your other friends. I've been trying to ask about your life for months, and you have said, 'Let's talk about you instead.'" When I returned home, she called me, mortified. I assured her her feelings were welcome. What I didn't say was I desired relationships where "messy" feelings were honored and worked through, but the attacks were something I didn't want anymore.

The next evening was my overnight flight to Puerto Rico. I had not flown Frontier Airlines in years, and their plastic seats made for an uncomfortable long flight from Denver. I arrived stiff, but the warm tropical breezes calmed my nervous system. I picked up the SUV I had rented and drove three women I picked up at the airport through the back country of Puerto Rico to our home for the long weekend on top of a hill overlooking the ocean. The view was stunning from the open-air home. The home showed signs it had not been inhabited since the hurricane that had devastated Puerto Rico a couple of years prior. This was a spiritual wealth coaching program, and my female classmates were not impressed. Water was dripping though the top floor, but hey, I had been to Ecuador, so it didn't bother me.

I enjoyed meeting Corrina in person. She was shorter than I imagined, but her presence was more powerful in person.

Before retiring, we gathered in the central room and Corrina led an opening ceremony with candles and sage. The next day, we visited the ocean for our first portal experience of three. The sand was terra cotta, heavy, and deep—my feet dropped several inches with each step. We were told to find a place that spoke to us. Finding my spot, I gazed into the portal at the horizon and sensed fairy dust emanating from my finger tips. I spent the rest of the day sensing the qualities of healing present in this energy. It felt like my fingers were emanating lightness and wondered if I could call on this at will.

I woke up the next morning and over our cups of coffee, I asked Corrina, "What kind of birds were singing last night?"

She replied, "They are frogs." I had never heard frogs who whistled and met one perched on my bathroom wall when I took my cold shower. He was so cute and tiny with bug eyes. Coqui frogs are considered sacred in Puerto Rico.

This day we were visiting a swimming hole in the rainforest. Corrina believes it is a gateway to another realm. We traveled to the beautiful El Yunque Forest and approached a bridge. Corrina stopped and said, "This is the opening of the portal," so that we could sense the difference in energy as we crossed the bridge.

Arriving at the swimming hole, I noticed the huge boulders scattered throughout. One classmate suggested I lay on one and receive the portal's[46] energy. I picked one I felt drawn to and lay down. As I closed my eyes, three angelic beings appeared to me, one after another. They were cloaked in light. Each glided toward me and paused for about a minute. I was neither asleep nor dreaming. Up until that moment, I was not particularly visual in my sensing, probably due to my poor eyesight since my childhood. I wore glasses in kindergarten. The sensing I developed was kinesthetic.[47] But these beings' faces are etched in my memory. My work with Connie was enhancing my ability to sense and see spirits.

Dare to Dream launched while I was there, and Paula joined us for a live launch. My trip to Puerto Rico was literally eye opening. *Was I seeing things?* I was questioning what was real anymore, but the experience piqued my interest in learning what portals were. My interest would evolve into a deep dive into all I could learn over the next couple of years. Through my studies, I would remember a gift, one I would learn to master.

"The wound is where the light enters you."

—Rumi

---

[46] *Portals* are metaphysical gateways or openings believed to connect different dimensions or realms of existence, often recognized in spiritual practices as sources for energy, guidance, and spiritual experiences.

[47] *Kinesthetic sensing* refers to the perception of body movement and position, often described as the "sixth sense," which enables awareness of muscles, joints, and balance. See Susan J. Lederman and Roberta L. Klatzky, "Hand Movements: A Window into Haptic Object Recognition," *Cognitive Psychology* 19, no. 3 (1987): 342–368.

6

My Initiation

T here were only a few days between my trips, so I loved up Greta when I returned, made sure she had her injections before Lea's return, and packed for Ecuador.

Having made the arrangements to take some time away from my coaching business for a few weeks, I boarded another flight to Quito. Luigia, my taxi driver, picked me up at the airport. She had driven us to and from our hotel on my first trip. Luigia doesn't speak English. After a couple of months of Spanish classes, I could say a few phrases. We had a joyful broken conversation, and she shared photos of her pets and sons. Everyone who takes care of me in Ecuador is so kind and loving. They all smile and laugh so much—I wasn't accustomed to that much joy in the US.

This second trip to Ecuador, I rejoined Tati and Monique, but for a different journey. The group was smaller—besides myself, only two men and a woman, all from the New York area. I met my fellow journeyers at the same hotel. This time, Tati met us at the hotel and took us to buy boots. *Something about a river?*

The next day we ventured to visit the shamans at their homes. Our first stop was Shairy's. He had built a fire and spoke of yin/feminine and yang/masculine energies and the importance of balancing these energies into oneness. After his talk, each one had a private session with him. It was my turn.

I ducked my head to enter the small opening of his igloo-shaped sanctuary crafted from a sand plaster. My bare feet created dust as I walked across the dirt floor to sit on a pillow across from him. His eyes twinkled with tenderness as he smiled and said, "Welcome, brother." We had met once before. Monique sat beside me, interpreting his Spanish with reverence and high-spirited animation.

I asked him many questions. Healing sounds and vibrations infused my cells with ancient wisdom as he sang, beat his drum, and blew Spirit through his flute. Instructing me to place a rock on top of my head, he asked me if I received a message.

I replied, "Total stillness."

"That is good," he said. He instructed me to stand barefoot on the earth each morning and place my hands on the top of my head, creating a cup-like opening. With my fingers outstretched to Source's energy from the Sun, I was to allow this energy to flow through my body and feet. I was learning to be a conduit.

Gazing into my eyes while holding my hands, he told me, "You are exactly who you are meant to be." After a moment of silence, he added, "And everything happens at precisely the right time." My quest to merge the wisdom of his two statements would require me to embody unconditional self-love, with the deep knowing that most things aren't up to me at all. I wasn't fully there, yet.

We embraced each other, and he said, "Hasta pronto!" (See you soon!)

The next morning, we boarded the bus to visit two more shamans in their homes. Ecuador has much poverty. The first "house" we arrived at looked like a house in its early stages of construction in the US. A basic structure of walls and a roof. As we entered the main room, we were met with dirt floors and a couple of wooden benches to sit on. An outhouse was down an open-air hallway.

Maria Juana greeted us with the biggest smile and a hug around my waist. She was a tiny round elderly woman with jet black hair dressed in traditional Ecuadorian clothes—a white blouse with bright colorful embroidery around the neck and short sleeves and a navy blue skirt with a similar stitched border around her waist and at the bottom. Every word she spoke was a prayer as she smiled, looking upwards.

There were piles of leaves that she and her son Raul were gathering into bunches. We were told to strip to our underwear. I was sensing this trip was going to be more primal and raw than my first. She prayed diligently to invoke spirits and facilitate the healing process as she whacked us with leaves to draw out negativity.

Raul came over to me and spit liquor all over my body. *Aguardiente* is liquor with herbs and is believed to remove negative energy, give blessings, and facilitate a transfer of power. I was experiencing a spiritual cleansing called a *limpia*. Raul also sucked energy off me and then ran to the bathroom and threw up. After this purification, Raul handed me a powerful spear and made me stand like a warrior and hold the spear against my chest. He instructed me to pound my chest and utter "Shunga, Shunga, Shunga." I felt stronger than I ever had. I hugged and thanked them both as we left their sacred home.

When we got back on the bus, I sat next to Monique, and she turned to me and said, "You know you were being initiated." I was still unclear what that meant.

The next day, we participated in another ten-hour sweat lodge ceremony. This time when Tati asked me to sing, I sang with more confidence. I sat next to Graham, a designer from New York City.

When the round of "cleansings" began, Graham asked if I could be a part of his cleansing.

Tati said sure. I was honored and I was throwing myself into an arena I had little knowledge about. I watched Monique and Tati tap feathers on Graham and blow on him, sending energy off his body. Tati handed me a stone and said, "Use this to pull energy out of Graham's body, then tap it on the earth to release it." I did that for several minutes, sensing areas where I felt excess energy. Then Monique held Graham from his back as he sunk into her body for support and started to shake. I sensed I was supposed to sit opposite him and send him strength and support. As we watched pain release from his solar plexus, I held his hands while Tati spit spirits on him. His body relaxed, and we held him as he regained his strength.

I didn't fully know what I was doing, but it felt powerful, and Graham thanked us and returned to his seat, renewed.

Don was next, and Monique sat down and gave me guidance at this time. I held Don as he sobbed. He needed to be held by a man. Monique gave me a feather, and I tapped it on different parts of his body. Monique asked, "Do you see that?" and I started to see what she was seeing—parts of his body seemed sunken. The feather gave those parts both comfort and energy.

After these *limpias*,[48] it was my turn.

Monique handed me a knife, and Tati poured water over me. They told me to stand on my knees. My body trembled, and I felt the urge to yell. Tati said, "Tell your ancestors what you are feeling; they need to know." I was so angry at their racism, colonization, and especially how my grandfathers treated me.

---

[48] *Limpias:* Traditional cleansing rituals in Mexican culture, often involving the use of herbs, prayers, and energetic techniques to remove negative energies and promote spiritual well-being.

As my yells faded, Monique said, "Now take back your power from your ancestors." I took several deep breaths with the knife on my heart. My heart was racing, and I needed to sit to integrate this experience.

After the ceremony ended, we crawled out of the lodge and I lay next to Tati as we gazed at the stars. As our bodies cooled, we started talking about Divine Masculine energy. It was a concept I was not familiar with. I, like many men, was more familiar with the disempowered masculinity of our culture with its abuse and put downs. Tati told me that one of her dogs had given birth to a new litter of puppies and how her male dog, the puppies' father, stood guard over them. He was protecting them, displaying a natural tendency to embody the Divine Masculine energy. Tati said protection is a main quality of the Divine Masculine, and we started naming other qualities and discussed how to bring its best qualities into our lives. Our conversation would continue through this trip and even after.

The next morning, we boarded our minibus and drove for seven hours toward our destination, which was quite mysterious. March, or Marzo in Spanish, is the beginning of the rainy season in Ecuador. As we drove in the pouring rain through the lush mountains, we crossed several washed-out roads. We arrived at one the bus driver said he could not drive over. The nearby overflowing river had a fierce current.

We sat in our seats in silence. After a few minutes, Tati said, "Put only what you need for the next couple of days in your back packs." Then she said, "Oh, and no lights." I thought, *But surely there will be outlets for our cell phones.* The uncertainty and not being able to contact anyone from the outside in case something happened became real.

A pickup truck appeared out of nowhere, and a young man dressed in a jersey and shorts loaded up our things. We crammed into the hatch back for the bumpy ride to somewhere.

It was dark when we arrived at the bamboo house on stilts nestled in the middle of the jungle. Chickens, big and small, were dashing in and out of the open door. An older man stood in front. His long gray hair was swaddled in a bun. He swatted at the chickens to come out of the house and turned to me and said, "I had more chickens, but an ocelot showed up last night and ate most of them." The thought of a midnight pee outside becoming fatal entered my mind.

There were two sweet dogs, one had just given birth to crying puppies, and a feisty little cat that lived inside. And there was the rooster. Little did I know, his perch was on the roof over my bed.

The man was a shaman named Bola. He didn't smile much as he greeted us and showed us to our rooms. As he opened the door to mine, I saw my bed for the next few days—a wooden platform bed with a very thin mattress and mosquito net, next to a table. He lit a candle and said, "Don't leave your bag open. There are 'many things' that will crawl inside." He then advised me to keep my door closed to prevent the bats from getting inside. With this information, my mind began creating images of what the "things" could be. Without the familiar anchor points of light, electricity, and hot water, I was beginning to feel far more vulnerable and raw than I had on my previous trip.

He graciously served us a warm vegetable soup for our dinner in the dark. Before an ayahuasca ceremony, eating only vegetables and fruit is the *dieta*.[49] A couple of candles on a large wooden dining table next to the kitchen made the large open room of the bamboo hut somewhat visible. After dinner, my flashlight guided me back to my room.

Very conscious of the possibility of encountering the "things," I quickly unzipped the mosquito net, then quickly zipped it as tight as I could and lay on my stiff wood bed. I didn't sleep much.

---

[49] *Dieta*: A traditional practice in certain Indigenous cultures, often involving fasting or abstaining from certain foods and behaviors, used for spiritual purification and preparation for shamanic experiences.

In the morning, I hobbled into the main room, sore from sleeping on wood, to join the others for our breakfast of tea and fruit, our *dieta*.

After breakfast, Tati, Monique, me, and the other journeyers were told to go to the open-air, dirt-floor basement by way of a series of steep wooden stairs. Clinging to a railing, I carefully took each precarious step down. Stepping on to the dirt floor, our cold showers and toilets, which we had to pour water into, were to my right, and a *temazcal*[50] was to my left.

Bola gave each of us bamboo poles to "get acquainted with" and told us to play with our weight and angles, as the poles would help us on a "hike." Though I had no context for why we were given these instructions, I followed them, twirling my pole, standing on one foot, extending my weightless leg with my body in various plank positions, and balancing my weight with partners. Had I known how much I was going to need to rely on these light sticks the next day, I would have been more focused on what this training was preparing me for.

As we gathered in a circle around the fiercely burning fire, we picked our pad and were given a plastic bag. This ceremony was much easier for me than my first—well, except for the cold dirt floor, chirping bugs, howling dogs, and the bugs crawling all over my skin. After I threw up, tiny angels wrapped a rainbow-plumed headdress around my crown and led me to a heavenly purple throne. I settled onto it, and the flowing energy of the medicine guided me gently, revealing places reminiscent of Nirvana and the Garden of Eden, full of lush greenery and breathtaking views. Waterfalls surrounded me, cascading through my very being. The water enveloped me in peace, joy, and wonder. (If only I had grasped what the next day's real-life journey to these same stunning natural treasures would involve!)

---

[50] A *temazcal* is a traditional Mesoamerican sweat lodge used for purification, healing, and ritual, typically constructed of stone or mud and heated with volcanic rocks. See John Bierhorst, *The Mythology of Mexico and Central America* (New York: William Morrow, 1990), 191.

When my mind tried to figure out where I was being led, the journey would stop. The shaman had said, "If you feel any discomfort, just focus on breathing through it." So, I began blowing away my thoughts and mind chatter and, as if by magic, I'd be brought back to those realms of beauty immediately. It enhanced the power of conscious breathing for me.

Thinking back on my conversation with Tati about the Divine Masculine, I grew curious about how I might experience it for myself. This desire to explore its qualities of protection and strength brought me to my intention for the ayahuasca ceremony with Bola—to connect with that sacred energy.

As I asked the medicine to help me connect with this energy, Bola sang an *icaro* called "Let Go into the Flow." As I sunk into my pad and surrendered to the medicine, my father appeared, encouraging me with the words, "Son, embrace the Divine Masculine. Feel the support that I could not provide fully." I relaxed deeply, letting go into this newfound sense of support, a pillar of strength and protection from the Divine Masculine. I had long yearned for this nurturing presence and support and had almost given up hope of experiencing it in my lifetime.

My relaxation gave way to a burning in my solar plexus at the end of the ceremony. I sensed there was still something stuck in my solar plexus that I hadn't released. I attempted to throw it up, but it lingered. I pondered this as we walked across the basement to the sweat lodge.

During the sweat lodge ceremony, Tati burned her arm badly on one of the rocks. The heat of the temazcal released my logical mind and connected me back to my heart and my feeling of gratitude for experiencing the support of the Divine Masculine. Having a taste of this Divine energy, I knew there was more to release in order to fully embody it.

After the ceremony, my limp body stumbled up the steep steps up to the main level, where my room was located. Rolling into bed, making sure to zip the mosquito net, I lay on the stiff wood, pondering what more I needed to release. It was impossible to sleep after a full night of ceremonies, and as my bed was situated directly under the rooster's, at dawn I abandoned all hope of sleeping. Dehydrated and sleep-deprived, my defenses were crumbling. After some morning relaxation, we faced a choice between a six-hour hike or a one-hour trek along a river to a waterfall and back. Our weary group chose the latter.

"Hike" hardly captures the experience that awaited us. Being the gentleman I am, I volunteered to carry the fruit container for our snack in my backpack. At the time, I was wholly unaware of how heavy it was and how much it would weigh me down.

So, with our knee-high rubber boots, we embarked on the one-hour "hike"—which turned into a six-hour slog through the jungle. Bola and Monique led, and Tati supported us from the rear. It was muggy, and my sunglasses fogged up. We headed up the hill in front of the Bola's house, and as we reached the top, I was already sweating profusely. I realized the other side was akin to a black diamond ski slope of mud. Straight down. It was the rainy season, and it had poured all night the evening we arrived.

Each step was treacherous. I slid down the hill, trying not to crash into the people ahead of me, which surely would have created an avalanche. Every branch I reached for detached from its tree. Nothing was solid. Having recently had my right hip and knee replaced from years of dancing, I was stable but not flexible. Slipping along with my boots tangled in vines, I galumphed down the steep muddy hill.

We reached a beautiful river whose swift, gushing current shot over the wobbly rocks we were supposed to balance on. As we traversed the river, I slipped and lost my bamboo pole. I watched the current devour it. With his machete, Bola sliced me a new pole, which was much heavier than the bamboo one I'd just lost. My boots filled with water, which made my feet heavy. With every step, my backpack grew heavier and heavier. Sweat poured down my face. I could barely see and was rapidly losing what little energy I had left.

We approached an enormous boulder covered in moss, and I watched Bola grab hanging vines, pulling himself across the slippery boulder. He teetered—his feet had less than an inch of a ledge to balance on. *I can't do that*, I thought. But I did. I still don't know how.

We turned a corner, and I saw the most stunning waterfall. Its powerful rush sent water cascading into a serene pool, the surface cool and inviting. I'd never appreciated cold water so much. The beauty of the place was so worth all the misery and effort it had taken to get there. We stopped for a break, and I collapsed on a slab of rock. When I handed my pack to one of the leaders, he said, "Gregorio, that is so heavy."

Tati turned to me. "I think there's something heavy you need to let go of." *Understatement.* I gave thanks and rested in the water, allowing the flow to heal me.

It was time to return. We had to go back over the terrain I could barely cross the first time. I thought, *I will never make it back.* I knew that if I looked too far ahead, I'd be terrified and lose any confidence I had left. So, I took baby steps and kept breathing. *Don't look too far ahead—stay present* was my mantra. Going up that hill was way more challenging than going down it had been. I couldn't get my footing in the mud. Everything I'd counted on was not working. Halfway up I said, "I need to stop. I can't go on. I need help."

Monique told me later, "Gregg, you went white."

Tati gave me coca leaf powder to suck on and liquid tobacco to snort. Monique gave me water to sip, and in about fifteen minutes, I could stand up again. Sort of. Bola instructed two young men to stand in front of and behind me and guide me with their bamboo poles. I leaned on them for the rest of the hike. I apologized to them, but both said, "You healed me in the sweat lodge, Gregg. Of course we will help you." Slowly, they guided my limp body back up that excruciatingly muddy hill.

The sound of Tati singing and whistling behind me calmed my restless mind and soothed my nervous system. I was grappling with the shame of being seen as weak. Each person was accessing their Divine Masculine energy, and they provided me unwavering support and protection. The Divine Masculine energy was empowering all of us with the strength necessary to return safely together.

When we made it back to Bola's house, I was soaking wet, covered in mud, and could barely stand. I collapsed on the bamboo floor. I lay there, raw and embarrassed. *What was that about?* I felt so exposed and vulnerable. I could not have made it back alone. Knowing I'd needed help and couldn't have navigated the path on my own was humbling.

I realized that I'd always protected myself by knowing everything that could possibly happen in any situation ahead of time—all so I could act appropriately and not get criticized. After the muddy hike to the waterfall, I understood that not only does the Universe support me; we are all interconnected, and we need each other on this journey of life. Each of my fellow journeyers had helped me at different times, and I didn't need to earn their help. As a caretaker, I'd always felt I had to give in order to receive, and this time, in the mud and the sweat and the exhaustion, I'd had nothing to give.

After we rested and I'd regained my strength, we gathered for an integration circle. Consumed by my own struggles, I failed to recognize that everyone around me had been facing their own challenges. As everyone shared their experience, a sense of immense gratitude enveloped me. Reflecting on how hard it was to be helped, I shared with the group that my parents were caretakers. Their traits had been passed to me, and I'd been living in a state of exhaustion for a long time. I'd invested everything I'd had in taking care of everyone else. I shared I'd truly believed I needed to do everything on my own. The hike brought revelations—Great Spirit was taking care of me. Yet I still couldn't meet everyone's eyes; there was a part of me that still felt powerless for needing help.

Discomfort in being seen as weak and needing help led me through an Initiation. Growth often emerges from discomfort, and this growth contributed to the process of retrieving my soul. Soul retrieval is a practice aimed at helping you reclaim lost parts of yourself, such as your vitality, power, and innocence, which can become lost when you fragment from your body.

We begin by using soul retrieval to address wounds from our childhood. We call back and retrieve those parts of our soul our inner child had to abandon to survive. As we continue this journey, we learn to recover our original essence—which embodies love and light and which knows how to talk to the animals, to the trees, and to Source.

Before the hike to the waterfall, I'd been asking for help from Spirit from a disconnected place. I'd believed I was only worthy of whatever scraps God served me. I'd believed that the best way to be humble was for God to pity me.

My second visit to Ecuador was a spiritual homecoming for me. In South America, the emphasis is placed on community rather than on the individual. When I am in Ecuador, I am welcomed into a family. My soul is home.

I noticed the contrast when I returned home to Colorado. It was beginning to feel like it wasn't home anymore. My neighborhood felt almost unfamiliar.

Integrating this experience, I was beginning to recognize that I had gifts, and they were from the Divine. This trip was me stepping deeper into my power as a leader. As I integrated these ancient practices into my daily life, I felt a deeper connection to the earth and to my soul.

Tati was supporting me, drawing on the synthesis of my life's journey—creating sacred healing art ceremonies with others. While aiming to integrate the ancient wisdom and confidence I was acquiring into the evolution of my shamanic journey, I reminisced about my thesis project, *Fluid*. I recalled the profound impact it had on everyone present in the room.

Holding this vision, I created an online workshop with Corrina's assistance. Frustrated by the lack of response I was receiving from it, I knew my heart was telling me these events needed to be in person to attain the deeper effect I was seeking. I also sensed I wasn't meant to do this by myself.

The next week, Kimberly and I began meeting online every week and over the next several months we began to co-create a retreat, Rejuvenate Your Radiance. She lives in beautiful Kauai, and we agreed the "Garden Island" was the perfect setting—the ocean, the warm sea breezes, the lush land of flowers and palm trees were rejuvenating on their own. We drew on our knowledge of the elements and movement to create a five-day retreat. Each day featured an element, and we created meditations, movements, and time in nature that corresponded with the element of the day. Offering fresh organic food, creating mandalas, and making leis were woven into the retreat.

We continued weekly meetings throughout the year, as we were offering the retreat in November.

Coinciding with this project, I received an email from Dr. DaeEss 1Drea Pennington, offering me an opportunity to write a chapter in her new book. Since the chapter I wrote in *Dare to Dream* was so powerful in my integration of my Kambo experience, I sensed I would gain clarity from my Ecuador experiences by writing about them.

Still, I felt a bit lost. It felt risky to reveal the person I was evolving into. I was no longer just a therapist; I was crafting an identity that I struggled to articulate to others, and even to myself.

There was a purpose calling me, revealing what I was here to do on earth, but I didn't know how I was going to bring it into the world.

"Every human is an artist. And this is the main
art that we have: the creation of our story."
—Don Miguel Ruiz

7

My Voice

Processing and integrating my life-altering journey, I re-read my Ecuador journal entries and continued to expand on them, adding details and elaborating on the experiences. I had always excelled in my university studies, receiving high marks for my writing, but I wasn't aware of how cathartic and therapeutic writing could be until I was given opportunities to write about my own experiences in these collaborative books.

Writing allowed me to make sense of the intangible—transforming feelings I couldn't quite express through movement or words in therapy into a narrative that articulated my pain and facilitated my growth. It helped me connect the dots between past traumas and present healing. Just as I had learned in my professional practice to open my body to receive messages from spirit, writing became another method to surrender and embody my soul. My second chapter was titled "Surrender to Spirit: Releasing Shame to Embody Leadership" for Dr. DaeEss 1Drea Pennington Wasio's book *Sacred Medicine*. In that chapter, I gave form to the spiritual experiences I had.

This was the tangible beginning of this book. The book I had in my head was beginning to take written form.

Return to New York

DaeEss 1Drea invited me to give a talk on my chapter at the Omega Institute in Rhinebeck, New York, and at a center for psychedelics in New York City. It was July, and my journey back to New York, where my spiritual path had begun, marked my first experience standing before an audience to share my personal story instead of portraying a character.

Returning to the home where I lived in the 1980s was surreal. New York had changed a lot, but its essence will always be loud and crowded for me. I checked into my midtown hotel and began not feeling well. Dizzy on the second night, I felt a message to throw up and spent much of the night in the bathroom. I was releasing bile, and it burned so much I lost my voice. *How am I going to give this talk?* I drank honey lemon tea the next day, and by the evening, my voice had returned.

The next morning, I boarded a train to the Hudson Valley. In these beautiful rolling hills of green a famous holistic camp is nestled. I arrived at the Omega Institute a couple of hours before my talk. The coordinator for speakers met me at the welcome house. She took me on a tour through the hilly terrain of the lush gardens, canopy trees, and wooden cabins in a golf cart.

When she dropped me back at the welcome house, my body was tingling all over, feeling a mix of excitement and fear. Outside on the woodsy Omega grounds, it was difficult for me to center myself and concentrate on practicing my presentation. The stimulation was too intense. I asked Spirit for help and was guided to take off my shoes, connect with the soft grass, and feel the grounding earth beneath me. Focusing on deep belly breathing, I directed my speech to the nearby stream. I felt nature's support profoundly—it reminded me of how the elements of nature had aided my healing journey in Ecuador.

When the time came to give the speech, I drew nature's calming energy into my heart and made my way to the presentation hall. DaeEss greeted me and smudged me; calling on Ram Dass's energy, she gave me a welcoming and gracious introduction. As I walked to the podium, I felt energized and connected with the audience. Rather than shying away from eye contact, as I had done in past presentations, I connected with the attendees, gazing into their eyes as I spoke. I noticed and heard them. The audience nodded when I asked the opening question, resonating with my story. I sensed that there was a greater force guiding my words. It was a healing experience for me. I felt myself releasing a deep layer of my fear of being seen.

My Talk

Have you ever been in a group or a class, and the teacher or leader asked you a question, and you froze? You couldn't find your breath, your mind went blank, and you couldn't find the words, but you knew you had them in your heart? I've suffered from not having words when called upon in learning circles since I was very young. In the chapter I wrote for Sacred Medicine called "Surrendering to Spirit: Releasing Shame to Embody Leadership," I share how sacred medicine helped me transcend this wound.

It's such an honor to be here in New York and to share my life-altering experiences with sacred medicine with you. I am again amazed by how the Universe has orchestrated this full-circle return to my home where I lived during most of the 1980s to give this talk. As a young man from the Midwest, I arrived here with $200 in hand to pursue an actor-singer-dancer-model career and never looked back.

New York sure has changed since then and it will always be the city to me where my deep spiritual journey began.

I saw my first therapist here and often attended her best friend's channeling of Emanuel in a church on the Upper West Side. It was here that I learned to meditate, where I first met my spiritual guide, Milton Sherman.

Milton is a little Liberace with a sparkling sequined jacket who rides a tiny pony. His job is to keep me light with his silly comments. This is where I had my first float tank experience. My first holotropic breathwork experience.

It was also where I attended my first Patti Labelle concert.

I sat enthralled as I witnessed what seemed to be her leaving her body and surrendering to spirit and trusting this divine orchestra of instruments flow through her all evening. There was no way that she could have rehearsed what she shared with us. She was surrendering and trusting something larger than herself, not knowing where these sounds were going.

I know this practice of surrender is inherent in gospel singers in African American churches throughout the US. It's often referred to as "they caught the holy ghost or spirit." Experiencing non-ordinary states was why I turned to my acting and performing talents to express the light within me, because it was safer to be someone else. By losing myself and letting Spirit move me, I relished in how my performances touched and affected audiences.

It was when my spiritual pursuit in New York City became more important to me than performing that I discovered how surrendering to spirit was not about losing myself, but finding my true self, and that is how I continue to heal myself and help others heal from our wounds and traumas.

So how do we surrender to Spirit?

We are divine souls on a sacred journey. We arrive as light, and then our society, parents, and family members, teachers, and other authority figures can dim that light with their words and actions.

You know you have a set of unique gifts and qualities that no one else in this world has, and they are meant to be shared with all of us. I believe that the journey of discovering, bringing to light, and expressing those gifts is each of our purposes in this life. Indigenous cultures have supported each person's unique expression for centuries, as they treat each seat in the circle of their ceremonies as essential to the attainment of the highest good for all concerned. It's one of the many reasons I have made two trips to Ecuador in the last year to experience the mysterious ancient wisdom of the sacred medicines of San Pedro and Ayahuasca that are native to that part of our world.

As I mentioned earlier, I was born with a divine light that was brilliant, uniquely creative, and innocent.

I shared the story of how my innocence had been stolen in kindergarten, when I wet my pants and was humiliated by my teacher and teased by my classmates.

As I boarded my flight to Quito, Ecuador, I wondered what my sacred journey had in store for me. I felt I was missing a skill as a healer. I heard that "Grandmother," what the indigenous people of South America call the plant medicine Ayahuasca, didn't give you what you wanted. Instead, she always gave you what you needed. I discovered the truth of that statement.

I went on to describe my first trip to Ecuador, focusing on being called by the shaman to sing in both the sweat lodge and the ayahuasca ceremony.

In sacred ceremonies, many of the themes of songs are the Spanish word corazón, which means "heart." It also means compassion and courage. Sacred medicine gives us the courage to access and live from the wisdom of our heart.

So, my answer to the question I posed to you earlier, "How do we surrender to spirit?" is that we find this courage to surrender to spirit in our hearts.

When we can welcome our wounds with love and compassion, breathe into them, and express and release our feelings fully, we always encounter an even deeper experience of the vibration of love on the other side of our pain and wounds.

So, if I could feel that amount of love, compassion, and forgiveness in my body with the medicine, I realized that this is my new set point. That it is possible to feel that in my daily life. To make the non-ordinary ordinary. So, I have made it my mission to assist as many willing souls as I can in releasing their wounds and in dissolving into who they truly are. Which is literally light. So, as we evolve into that light, we are taking part in the evolution of our species. And I can't think of a better purpose than that.

After their applause, several of the audience members approached me smiling, relating to my wound. On our walk to the Omega bookstore for the book signing, a woman from the audience wanted to know more about my work. I shared my somatic practices with her, as the ancient wisdom I was learning hadn't fully integrated into my professional life . The taxi driver waited for me to finish and drove me back to my hotel. From the back of the taxi, I was gleaming, softly. I had done it—spoken in front of an audience authentically as myself, not a character, with a little showmanship, of course. I slept really well and the next morning, I caught the train to Grand Central Station. I had a few hours to rest in my hotel room before walking through a light summer rain to the Athenaeum for my next talk and book signing.

The Athenaeum is a member-supported social club, library, bookstore, and cafe dedicated to the conversation and education around psychedelics. I was joined by four of the other authors, and three of us were giving a talk. Susanne, my friend from Heartwood, had taken the subway in from Brooklyn to see me. It had been over thirty years since we had seen each other. We squeezed each other and shared a few memories. *There's that laugh again.* It warmed my heart and meant so much to me she was there. A photographer from London was taking shots from every angle as 1Drea greeted the crowd and began to introduce the first speaker.

The room was very humid from the rain and no air conditioning. I paced around, wiping the sweat from my forehead as I rehearsed my talk in my mind. When 1Drea introduced me as the next speaker, I froze for a second, took a deep breath, and walked up the steps to the stage. As I gazed down at the audience, my mind went blank. I surrendered to the moment, and the talk flowed through me effortlessly.

After our talks, the three of us gathered on the stage to answer questions from the audience. The last question I received was, "How has writing and speaking about your chapter affected your path forward?"

Without thought, "I feel guided to lead ayahuasca ceremonies" slipped out of my mouth. Stunned, I realized the implications of my words. I was a sixty-three-year-old white man who had two ayahuasca experiences. I knew I wasn't one of the Westerners who thought they could be a shaman and I didn't want to be seen as appropriating[51] the Andean culture.

I held too much respect for the elders who held the ancient wisdom, yet I knew I wanted to develop a deeper relationship with Grandmother.

Finding My Voice

When I found my path, I found my voice.

When you find your voice, when someone can see you or hear you, it brings so much joy and fulfillment. How I arrived there was with sacred medicine. My first Ayahuasca experience seemed to release more of my

---

[51] *Cultural appropriation* takes place when a dominant culture adopts aspects of a minority culture, frequently without proper understanding, permission, or acknowledgment. This practice can be seen as exploitative and disrespectful, as it removes cultural elements from their original meaning and perpetuates existing power imbalances.

wounding in a single night than I could with all the other modalities I had tried over the past thirty years. Sacred medicine held me until I could embody my voice and leadership.

My trip to Omega and New York City was a turning point in my career. I learned not only could I present to a live audience—I wanted to. Writing my truth and sharing my adventures and lessons with live audiences had opened the door to a new way of being for me, and I never looked back.

Reflecting on my surprising revelation to the audience in New York City during the flight home, I couldn't shake the feeling that I was too old to embark on the years of training needed to master the art of leading a sacred ceremony. When I landed back home, I reached out to Tati and headed back to Ecuador again, this time in septiembre.

"The Universe is circles within circles, and everything is one circle,
and all the circles are connected to each other."
—Black Elk

8

Life as a Ceremony

The main reason I am drawn to experience and study indigenous ways is that the people see Spirit in everything. Their wisdom lies in their interconnectedness with their territory, the plants, nonphysical beings, and the elements, and they believe each one bears ancient wisdom, which draws us human beings into our hearts.

One of the countless reasons I cherish taking part in sacred ceremonies is the opportunity to play my drum, sing, and heal alongside others. Praying and praising the Great Spirit with others enhances what I can accomplish alone. Instruments, such as rattles, drums, bowls, and gongs, in the ceremony shift vibrations, transforming the energy of the room and our bodies. We can tune into the profound frequencies of the Earth. Just as sunlight nourishes all life, healing sound frequencies nourish our souls, aligning our hearts with the universe's song.

Luigia picked me up at the airport as usual. My Spanish was a little better, and she simply giggled when she didn't understand me as we drove through the dark again. When I arrived at Hotel Casa Sayu at 1:00 a.m., Paticia, with her kind smile and her dog Chunky, wagging his tail, opened the gate and graciously greeted me and then walked me to my room for the week.

After a short sleep, I had the morning to rest and acclimate. Upon awakening, I walked through the groves of avocado trees and soaked up the warm Ecuadorian sun.

When I arrived at Tati's house, Maria, her housekeeper, opened the dark blue metal door with her usual sweet smile. Tati was in the kitchen, and after an *abrazo grande* (a big hug), we continued our conversations about how the Divine Masculine energy offers protection, support, and the courage to make new choices, while the Divine Feminine energy nurtures compassion and surrenders to spirit and flow. When they are woven together, there is balance, wholeness, and health. Unbeknownst to Tati and me at the time, our conversations were the spark that ignited our creativity and motivated us to create a retreat we would lead together in a couple of years.

Arriving at Tati's home, I felt a mixture of excitement and unworthiness. My intention has always been to honor the traditions with deep respect, so I approached this opportunity with great humility. When we talked about me learning these ancient ways, Tati reassured me I had asked her in the right manner, which granted me the permission I needed to explore further.

I brought my elk skin drum for this trip. I'd been asked to drum during the plant medicine ceremonies, and while for many years I'd owned a drum, I couldn't embrace playing it. Tati suggested that I use a felt-tipped mallet to enhance the vibration of my drum, so I picked one from her collection. I realize this was an essential part of making my drum my own—choosing what connected my hand and heart to the drum.

My Training

This was a personal teaching retreat for me. Tati guided me in the ancient wisdom of her Andean culture and taught me firsthand about the elements of ceremony and how to tolerate and remain present with the potent medicines. As she would say, "You are learning how to stay awake with the 'dizziness.'" It was a week full of beautiful ceremonies, each teaching me deep truths, and different people joined us at each ceremony.

The first ceremony was with mushrooms, and we gathered at the fire pit across from the sweat lodge. Tati's partner, Gallo, joined us. This ceremony taught me the importance of creating the sacred space with altars,[52] and how to open the portal for a ceremony. A beautiful altar of fresh flowers, bowls of water, and ancient figurines was placed at the entrance and against the rock wall on the opposite side. These physical portals served as containers, supporting the opening of the spiritual gateway to honor the spirits joining us in the ceremony. I was being taught about their specific placements and significance.

Anchors prepare the container and ceremony for what's coming. Every element—earth, air, fire, water—has as a role, an anchor for precise guidance from the spiritual realm. The portals invited spirits of light to enter and provide guidance. I learned to honor the importance of this alignment of the altars to pay tribute to the spirits. We had to prepare the ceremonial space precisely to receive the wisdom and guidance from the spirit realm.

Tati opened the portal by calling in the directions. She began talking about what the fire represented, and all of a sudden, a strong burst of wind blasted the fire out. It was not the weather. Curious, Tati turned towards the direction of this force and began talking to the spirits she perceived.

After she finished, I asked her about the altar, what each object represented, and why they were placed where they were. As she began pointing at a figurine, she froze, noticing a bowl of water was missing. Tati turned to Gallo and asked where it was. He had moved it. She asked why he had done this and explained this was the reason for the strong burst. Tati was speaking in Spanish, so I didn't understand each word, but I felt the

---

[52] An *altar* is a sacred space or platform used for religious or spiritual rituals, where offerings, prayers, or meditative practices are performed, often serving as a focal point for connecting with the divine.

intensity of them. The reality that there are greater forces at play became visceral for me.

Our ceremony shifted from focusing on fire to honoring water—what was called for beyond anyone's personal intentions. Many things are not up to us at all. It was in this ceremony that I learned how to navigate the world of forces.

Spirit Guides

In the second ceremony, two women from Quito joined us for a San Pedro and mushroom[53] ceremony. We again gathered in the fire pit. One of the women had brought beautiful purple roses, and she placed them in the center, where the fire normally is, with a bowl of water. As water served as the central element of this ceremony, the two women expressed their emotions through tears. Although I couldn't comprehend their Spanish words, I felt their sadness resonate deeply within my heart. They expressed their gratitude for my support and mentioned how much they appreciated my strength.

As I leaned back and looked up, I saw my spiritual support team, my guides. They were all sitting in a circle above my head, jumping up and down—celebrating and cheering me on. They were so happy to see me. I had not been connected to my spirit guide Milton consistently after meeting him in New York, so I reintroduced myself. My nonphysical guides became accessible to me at that moment and were eager and willing to help. I just needed to ask for it.

I felt a deep sense of gratitude and joy, knowing this was the main reason I came on this trip—to not only see spirits but to relate to them.

---

[53] *Psilocybin* is a naturally occurring psychedelic compound found in certain species of mushrooms, known for its mind-altering effects and potential therapeutic applications in mental health.

I slept like a baby that night and was able to sleep in the next morning in preparation for the ayahuasca ceremony that evening.

Grandmother Ceremony

I arrived at Tatis' mid-afternoon and met the shaman, Mercedes. There were only the three of us for this ceremony, which felt more like a conversation. Mercedes was beautiful, like a model—her shoulder-length brown hair caressed her perfect skin. She wore a thin white blouse, which exposed her round belly—she was pregnant.

She played the harmonica and served me various strains of the medicine. My first cup was intended for the spirit, and it filled me with a sense of joy. The second cup connected with the body, and I experienced a purging. Like I did on my first trip, I was releasing from my sacrum and receiving the light to fill that opening, which allowed unconditional love to fill me.

Mercedes said I was to work with the body as the gateway for others to transcend. Medicine, like breath, brings me into my body and amplifies what I must let go in order to transcend. This was my process, and it confirmed why my life's path took me to dance and somatic work to develop my sensing. My resonance with the process of guiding others in going within the body to access and release the wounds was deepening.

At that point, I excused myself to go to the restroom. On my walk outside, Grandmother spoke to me about becoming the water, to release with ease and grace. She told me to let go like the water instead of forcing a release. To relax my body to discover where there was holding and restriction. The more you force, the more you hinder the healing process. She encouraged me to embrace the journey of gentle unwinding, especially in times of discomfort. Water was teaching me to be gentle and compassionate with my releases.

Release Gently

Water became the element I was to connect with and learn from on this trip. The qualities of flow and ease. The wisdom of water was changing the way I related to myself and others. I discovered that attempting to force a release isn't effective. My challenges need to be nurtured to be freed. By embracing all aspects of myself, I could transcend my challenges. Sometimes a shift takes a day, a year, or even a lifetime to embody. Compassion allows the pain to flow from us with ease.

I recalled when I was a young therapist in California and Colorado, we forced expansions, pressing on body parts to achieve a result. We were always well meaning, but it pushed some people too far. I realized my work wanted to shift.

As we closed our intimate ceremony, my heart was full. I turned to Mercedes and said, "Being a mother is a miracle. So many of us take this miracle for granted. Thank you for all of the care you are giving your baby."

She bowed her head and said, "Muchas gracias." Mercedes gave me a bottle of ayahuasca for my trip home to begin microdosing in order to be acquainted with Grandmother's energy.

My last evening, we visited Tati's teacher, Avelina. Her eyes glowed with ancient wisdom as she welcomed us and invited us into her small home. She was interviewing people for her book about Neo-Shamans—Westerners who incorporate elements of ancient wisdom, psychotherapeutic techniques, and New Age spirituality. During our interview, I told her,

"When I stay embodied in the spiritual realm, I return with enhanced senses, especially to subtle energies."

She said, "That is good!"

Then I asked her, "I feel that I am supposed to bring the wisdom I gain in ceremony to the world."

She said, "Yes. It is your duty to bring wisdom back by becoming a bridge from the spiritual world to the physical world." Avelina walked us to Tati's car, hugged me, and smiled. "Hasta pronto." *See you soon.*

We ended my training in a sweat lodge with the community. I sang again and spoke a little Spanish. Tati didn't translate much for me this time. In Ecuador we say, "Ajo metakuyasi oyasin" when we open the flap door of the sweat lodge, sending our healing and prayer out into the Universe, intending to create a ripple effect. The Lakota phrase translates to "all my relations," expressing the interconnectedness of all living things and the universe.

We enjoyed a feast of fresh fruit, and then Tati and I joined her mother and son Azule for our traditional final meal of *Maito de Pescado*—seafood, plantains, and rice wrapped in banana leaves and cooked over an open fire.

My training was full, and my mind and belly were stuffed, but my heart remembered everything.

The next morning, before my flight home, I met Tati in her office to integrate our week of ceremonies and training. Tati told me she lived each day as a ceremony. She prayed, called in the directions, and asked the spirits for guidance for her day.

Placing a green piece of paper on the table, she handed me a bowl of random objects—strings, clay Ecuadorian figurines, talismans, stones, and beads. She invited me to pick one object that represented those whom I wanted to invite to my workshop, one object that represented what I wanted to teach, and three to represent the skills I would use.

Then she placed a blue piece of paper on the table, and I repeated the exercise. Now I was to go home and discover what I wanted to create.

I was beyond grateful. I had developed a deeper connection with my drum and felt worthy of beating it. I met my spiritual support team, learned about portals and altars, and gained wisdom from water to not force but rather allow life to unfold. In order to lead ceremonies, I would follow Tati's example, creating personal ceremonies. Calling in the directions with my guides each day would guide me.

This was just the beginning of a new chapter in my healing journey—one that would take me even further into the mysteries of the spirit.

"The person who set out on the journey
is not the person who arrives."
—David Whyte

9

Weaving Conscious Embodiment and Ceremony

Upon returning home, I felt a surge of motivation to embrace this new version of myself and explore how I wanted to engage with the world. As I wove the wisdom I had gained into my everyday life, the real work began.

In Ecuador, after a ceremonial experience, we begin to integrate our transformational healing by connecting with nature through a hike, which offers an embodied approach supported by the elements. However, true transformation occurs when we return to our homes and cultural environments and integrate what we've learned. One key function of integration is to stabilize our newly awakened spiritual consciousness. Although expanded states of consciousness can be challenging to incorporate into everyday routines, they hold tremendous creative potential for positive transformation.

The day after I returned, Tati called and invited me to connect with the directions to enhance the opening to the spiritual realm that I had experienced with her. Invoking the directions is a personal prayer, often marking the start and conclusion of ceremonies. Each direction has an animal totem whose wisdom uplifts us, offering guidance that inspires us to remember and uphold the healing container of the ceremony.

Weaving Ancient Wisdom with Somatic Practices

The directions guide my pure potential, supporting and reminding me what is most important and true. I spent a week meditating on the East and receiving guidance. The next week, the South, then on to the West and North.

East

Home of the Eagle, the Place of Clarity and Illumination

> *Prayer: Illuminate my path and give me the courage and freedom so I may fly like the eagle to the light.*

South

Home of the Coyote and Our Inner Child

> *Prayer: Remind me of the wonder and innocence of my Inner Child and help me remember my childlike qualities so that I may restore my joy and experience the magic in my life.*

West

Home of the Bear, Introspection, and Trust

> *Prayer: Help me enter the silence and look within to find my inner strength and guidance.*

North

Home of the White Buffalo, Wisdom, and Gratitude

> *Prayer: There are no limitations when I reach wisdom. I am grateful for new understandings and the many blessings of great mystery.*

The next month I focused on my assignment from Tati—integrating the knowledge I'd gleaned from being a dancer, massage therapist, and somatic psychotherapist using the tools of meditation, conscious breathing, movement, and voice into a sacred circle container.

Initially, Depth Integration was a downloaded aspiration. It was a practice in conscious embodiment. These were the methods I learned in my life and studies that I could create my new work from. My task was weaving the ancient wisdom I was learning in Ecuador into a tapestry for myself and others. Integrating these common threads that Kimberly and I shared was creating a beautiful retreat, and we started receiving interest from possible participants to join us in a couple of months.

So what are the common themes of Conscious Embodiment and indigenous wisdom that aid in healing and transformation? I began to ask myself.

The Power of Deep Relaxation

After I quit my job, living and working from home, I was benefiting from slowing down and relaxing. As I slept more, my nervous system began to let go of stress of the fast-paced world I had worked in. Stress was a significant contributor to my physical, emotional, and mental challenges. My chronic pain, lack of purpose, and illness stemmed from imbalances in my life. Relaxing deeply not only lowered my blood pressure and heart rate; I began to lose weight and quit drinking wine every night. I was sensing not only my inner experience but the energies outside my body and began to interact with them.

Relaxing deeply is encouraged in ceremony and in receiving guidance from the spiritual realm. Experiencing this connection was more profound once I had gone through therapy. Years of therapy prepared me for what I was diving into. I realized, however, that therapy had a set of skills that helped me progress, but they only took me so far.

The healing I encountered in Ecuador was deeper than I had experienced in my psychological training. Kimberly felt the same way from her travels to Africa. In Kimberly's work, Rainbow Light, she also helps others connect with their spiritual support team. I was so excited to have her weave this element into our retreat, as I was connecting with my team now. Our collaboration was also helping me define my new work.

Ceremony

When I began asking for help from my guides, the directions, and the animals, my sessions became ceremonies. Tati's advice guided me to create each day as a ceremony.

I began integrating the ancient wisdom I had learned. By staying connected to Great Spirit and my guides, every day, every thought, every action, and every interaction became a sacred ceremony of many rituals. I began each day sitting by my altar, communing with all beings and elements, past and present, expressing gratitude for my many blessings, smudging my body with sage, and cleansing my energy.

I asked my guides, the directions, and Great Spirit questions. "How may I be of service today?" In appreciation for their help and guidance, in sacred reciprocity, I gave them gifts of honey and flowers on the earth.

Not only did I connect with the themes, prayers, and animals of the directions; new guides appeared when I opened the portal to meditate: Anselmo held the fire stick below me—his name means *God's protector*. Camilla poured sacred water in my mother's honor—her name means *priest helper, attendant in a ceremony*. Guillermo, my spiritual warrior brother and protector, sat beside me. Satori—meaning *awakening, seeing into true nature*—sat in front of me. A hawk rested on my right shoulder, a crow on my left. An eagle perched on my head, and a snake coiled in front of my sacrum. Angelique arrived first, a messenger of God; she's a fairy who sprinkles fairy dust on me, the sprinkles waking me every day.

Their presence comforts me—they are my spiritual support team. Truly, I am not crazy, but as Shairy said, "You walk in two worlds."

It was creating a sacred space for Source, my spirit guides, and the spirit of the earth. Sitting at my altar, I recalled that in Ecuador, I'd become proficient at creating this space for others and now I was doing it for myself.

I closed each ceremony by giving thanks and gratitude.

My intense focus over the past few months had been in solitude. I didn't have much contact with the outside world except for Kimberly.

Out of the blue, my brother called me from Missouri. During our chat, he told me he felt that our mother shouldn't drive anymore, but she wouldn't listen to him. She was suffering from macular degeneration and had lived alone since my father passed away six years ago. I had been away for forty years and sensed I should move to Missouri.

What about my work? I thought. Leaving Colorado, where I had lived for over thirty years, made little sense to my mind, but my inner voice often communicates not through words but through my felt sense and the silent language of my heart. It embodies the essence of truth for me. So, over the next couple of months, Lea helped me sell many of my belongings and I put my place on the market. It all happened so quickly, as if another force was guiding the process.

My friend Nancy had recently shared with me that she was facing a serious illness. I tried to support her by checking in frequently and offering assistance, yet I still felt as if I was walking on eggshells. In hindsight, I wish I had been brave enough to share my true feelings with her; however, I didn't want to burden her with my emotions while she was already coping with so much. Instead, I expressed my gratitude for her generous spirit and sent her well wishes via text—a decision I now wish I could change. Everything felt so overwhelming and rushed.

October quickly turned to November, and despite feeling rushed, I intended to close this chapter of my life with gratitude—for Colorado, my home and my dear friends. I created several personal ceremonies giving thanks to the mountains and to my home for having held me in peace and beauty for many years.

Tati had given me two blocks of ceremonial cacao from Ecuador, and this felt like the right time to use them to honor Annette and Lea. Cacao, the raw form of chocolate, is a beautiful heart-opening medicine. First I went to Annette's home. As we sipped the cacao, tears streamed down our faces. We reminisced about our trips together, our friends and family whom we shared time with, and our deep connection with our pets, Chubba and Calli (her Frenchies) and Harry and Greta, my cats. We were family—their special aunts and uncles.

It was an overcast late autumn Sunday when Auntie Lea arrived for a ceremony honoring our deep love for each other and Greta. It brought me immense comfort to know that Greta was deeply loved and well cared for during my absence, surrounded by such unwavering devotion.

Greta was snuggled in a blanket on my bed. When the cacao was warm, I invited Lea into my living room where I had created a sacred altar with two zafus for us to sit on. As I lit the candle and opened the portal, suddenly Greta appeared and jumped on the chair next to Lea. Settling into a sphinx-like pose, she closed her eyes and joined the ceremony. Lea and I looked at each other in amazement and broke into tears; over the years, we both were enchanted by Greta's awareness and love. Greta not only knew she was the focal point of our ceremony, but she was expressing her gratitude to Lea. It was through Greta our love for each other grew.

Although I felt grief leaving Lea, the gratitude for the care she gave Greta and the love we shared was stronger.

It was a week before our *Rejuvenate Your Radiance* retreat when Kimberly and I solemnly joined on a call. While there was a lot of interest, we didn't have enough people sign up. We had to cancel our retreat.

Insecure thoughts began to rise: *Am I supposed to be doing this? Was quitting my secure job a mistake? Is this really my calling?* But there was this voice inside that said, *Keep going.* Monique, Tati, 1Drea, and Kimberly could see me leading, and receiving their support helped me retrieve my resilience. I felt so grateful these beautiful women saw something in me that I didn't fully own, yet.

My brother arrived mid-December to help me pack and load all my possessions into a moving truck he had driven to Colorado. He's also a skilled craftsman and he helped me paint and prepare my condo to sell.

A few days prior to my departure, a man from England, Barry, scheduled a discovery call for coaching with me for the day before I was scheduled to leave. For what seemed like an hour, we just looked into each other's eyes and smiled. He glowed, and I sensed a luminous energy surrounding him, which enveloped us. No time, no space. Barry told me he read my words and felt guided to reach out. Our connection was not about coaching.

Sometimes people like Barry come into my life, and there is an instant knowing, an instant connection. Source had brought us together for a Divine reason—and we would soon discover what that reason was.

The next day, my cat, Greta, and I, with the help of my brother, embarked on our new adventure. We set off for our new lives in my childhood home in Missouri.

"Still, I rise."

— Maya Angelou

10

Divine Light, Love, Will, Wisdom, and Power

G reta rode shotgun with me for the long flat drive through Kansas to Missouri, and about ten hours later, we arrived at the house I'd grown up in since third grade. It was a few days before Christmas, and my mom was so happy to see me after worrying about our drive. Another issue on both of our minds was how to introduce Greta to Oscar, her dog. Greta was now barely six pounds and fragile from her kidney disease, and Oscar was a strong seventy-pound boxer mix. Oscar was very respectful of his new guest, and we soon found out who was in charge—little Greta. Oscar was terrified to go up the stairs if she was sitting on one. He literally would not even attempt to. Greta was very powerful, even with her illness.

My days were spent taking care of Greta, and shortly after I arrived, my mother began experiencing severe nerve pain in her right leg, rendering her nearly immobile. Mom's pain was immense, and it was heart-rending to see her like that. I changed her diapers, dressed her, and cooked her meals. I took on the role of her caregiver for her, as well.

Between my duties, I had to unpack. I arranged my sacred space and office and set up my altars in the bedroom where my father had passed away. One day, while sitting at my desk, I was writing in my journal about my commitment to myself to break the voyeur cycle of mindlessly scrolling through sexual images whenever I felt vulnerable—a habit that was trapping me in shame. I felt with all of the work I did on myself, I should have healed this behavior by now.

Taking a break from my writing, I glanced over at a closet, and a lightning bolt struck me: that was the closet where I'd discovered the *Playboy* magazines in junior high. In that moment, my heart recognized that Dad's secret he was hiding in his closet, which I had internalized, wasn't solely mine.

Walking over to my altar, I lit a candle. I handed my secret side back to my father and the universe, releasing it into the flame, healing this ancestral, collective wound. Returning to the location where my adolescent secret had originated had become a crucial part of my journey of letting go of what didn't belong to me. After concealing that deep-rooted secret for so many years, a sense of relief washed over me. The veil of secrecy between me and others lifted, and I no longer felt the urge to hide out of fear of its discovery. Instead, I experienced a sense of genuine coherence with my true self that felt like a first in my life.

This coherence was further fostered in a year-long cohort I joined at the suggestion of my new friend Barry. He connected me to Dr. Lorna Collins, a spiritual mentor, who has developed a path of spirituality called Sourceness.[54] The cohort, co-taught by Louise Hansell, was a vital source of support for me during this transition of moving to my mother's house and in my personal and professional spiritual development.

---

[54] *Sourceness* is a concept in holistic health and spirituality that refers to a state of being connected to one's true self and the source of one's inner power and creativity. Source is the ultimate origin or foundation of existence, often conceptualized as a divine entity or force, regarded as the creator and sustainer of the universe in various religious and philosophical traditions.

During the cohort, I dove deep into the curriculum. Some of the teachings I knew from my studies, and others were new concepts and exercises which expanded my consciousness and were the answers I was looking for to embody the Divine—my life's quest.

Affirmations and Intentions

In the cohort, I revisited the power of affirmations[55] and intentions[56] from my exposure to Louise Hay and the Hendricks' work. I must confess that I was a skeptic of affirmations. When I didn't see immediate results, I thought to myself, *They don't work; they aren't real.* I was waiting for the effects until I realized affirmations help to uncover misalignments within myself that require healing.

Affirmations help reprogram my subconscious and clear emotional blocks. My consistent practice anchored my intentions as I explored the quantum field. In class, I sat on my throne of divinity, sovereignty, and power to connect with this field through my higher heart, using intentions to navigate effectively. While affirmations are vital, false positivity can harm by masking genuine emotions, leading to unresolved pain and chronic issues. Elevated emotions without somatic coherence are unsustainable. My morning ritual is essential for maintaining alignment with Source, allowing me to confront and release anything hindering my embodiment of unconditional love.

The foundation of teachings focused on cultivating and embodying five essential aspects of the Divine: divine light, love, will, wisdom, and power.

---

[55] An *affirmation* is a positive statement or declaration that reinforces a belief or intention, commonly used in self-help and psychological practices to promote personal growth, self-esteem, and mindset shifts.

[56] An *intention* is a focused and purposeful mental commitment towards achieving a specific outcome or goal, often emphasized in spiritual practices as a means of manifesting desires and aligning actions with one's true purpose.

Mantras

We began most exercises by repeating the Soul mantra three times. Mantras are like affirmations with the added dimension of invocation.

The Soul Mantra

I Am The Soul
I Am The Light Divine
I Am Love Divine
I Am Wisdom Divine
I Am Power Divine
I Am Will Divine
I Am Divine Design

The Soul Mantra invokes a shift in consciousness from self to the divine. Repeating this mantra daily instills my intention to embody the Divine.

Divine Power

Love had always come naturally to me, nurtured by the abundant love I received from my parents. However, I realized that love devoid of power can feel rather listless. My love had been sweet and other focused.

Returning to the location where my adolescent secret had originated had become a crucial part of my journey of letting go of what doesn't belong to me, but here was more to release into the flame. I had not completely released my urge to scroll and procrastinate. This urge continued to present itself, and I realized that giving it back with just love wasn't enough to release this habit. The shame I carried was difficult to acknowledge, accept, and approach with compassion. However, I realized that to truly let go, I needed to do so from a position of strength. I had to weave command with my compassion.

The essential qualities of strength and power had eluded me much of my life. I grasped for them outside of myself. In my efforts to embrace these qualities, I often pushed aside my vulnerability, which trapped me in a cycle of feeling powerless. My vulnerability was crying out to be embraced. I needed to love that part of myself and I found that challenging.

Following one of our group sessions, focusing on Divine power, the realization that power was actually a Divine energy took away my desire to look for it outside of myself. This internal knowingness that the energy of power was not mine personally made the act of opening and receiving Divine power effortless because it was a Divine energy, not something I had to muster. Power wasn't actually mine; it was much bigger than me. Almost instantly, the shift in awareness transformed my life experience.

The Staff of Divine Power

I had the opportunity to experience that Divine power a few weeks later when I took part in a retreat with Monique. Toward the end of our first day, Monique intuitively encouraged me to take hold of a remarkable staff adorned with crystals and feathers at its top. The energy it radiated was so intense that my hands trembled as I tried to grasp it. The trembling in my hands radiated into my arms and down my body. I shook and teetered, almost losing my balance. As I continued to connect with the staff and breathed, I sensed the crystals at the top were absorbing power from Source. Allowing my hands to relax, I merged with this powerful energy and became it.

When I returned to my mother's house, I shared this experience with Lorna and Louise, and they guided me to connect with the staff's energy in my meditations. I didn't need the physical divination tool because I could still feel the energetic strength of that staff. I became one with it, creating an everlasting bond between us. We connect often.

I needed this divine strength to sustain this new me, free of shame; one who no longer needed to hide. The next time the urge to scroll surfaced, I connected with the Divine power as I held my heart, and the energy of the urge began melting away. A warmth rose in my body as I accessed the power to give my shame my unconditional love. I was taking my power back to love my vulnerability and now didn't need a partner to support me in my vulnerability. Divine Light, love, and power were working in synergy.

This power sustained me not only in conquering my habit but in continuing to take care of Greta and Mom.

Greta continued to fail. She wasn't benefiting from the injections anymore. Mom's pain continued to worsen, and several doctors made the wrong diagnosis. Frustrated and beginning to lose hope, we met with a neurosurgeon who looked at all of the x-rays and reports and interviewed her. After the appointment, convinced her hip was the issue, he scheduled her hip surgery for June, which was a couple months away.

Greta – Being Love

On April 8, 2024, during a powerful eclipse, my teacher of divine love, my cat Greta, left her physical body. I had created a sacred altar on the green grass beneath a tall tree, whose anchored roots created the portal for her ceremony. Tears streaming down my cheeks, holding her body against my chest tightly, I beat my drum and sang the sacred song of the eagle to carry her soul from her limp body to the stars as she gasped her last breath.

The morning after, as I was meditating by the ceremonial tree, I gazed up to the sky just as a hawk flew over. I felt comforted by this messenger. I knew she was no longer in pain. What a blessing. While I miss her sweet little head resting on my arm as we meditated or slept, her teaching me to love unconditionally transformed me.

My most influential teachers of this life came in many forms, shapes, and sizes. Greta was tiny in stature, with a vast, loving presence. The epitome of a lap kitty, I always found that staring into her stunning blue eyes was a mystical experience. She exuded pure light. She embodied unconditional love so completely, it was impossible not to love her. She didn't have to give love; she was love. Her Auntie Lea aptly named her, "My Little Angel." Greta taught me I can't attempt to give or receive Divine love; rather, I am to be divine love with every cell of my body and soul, as she was. Integrating the depth of my beautiful little teacher's example of being Divine Love has been a daily practice in each present moment.

A couple of days after Greta's ceremony, I returned to Monique's. Tati was visiting her, leading ceremonies and giving private healings. The afternoon I arrived I had a private session with Tati, and she noticed a big shift in my energy since we last saw each other almost a year ago. Tati said, "I see you leading groups with another person." She then said, "Would you help me with the tobacco ceremony tomorrow?" I felt honored and wasn't sure what to expect.

The next day we gathered at the retreat center nestled in the rolling hills of upstate New York. A large group of thirty women and two men were in attendance. Tati teaches by example, not with direct instruction; I just had to jump in. After the first round of snorting liquid tobacco, Tati and Monique conducted the first individual cleansing in the middle of the circle. Several women had formed a line in front of me to be saged. I looked at Monique, and she motioned for me to go ahead. I had cleansed myself before but not others. I searched for the sage at the altar, picked a feather, and began saging each woman in line.

After the second round of passing and snorting the liquid tobacco, it was time for the second cleansing. Tati turned to me and motioned at me to join her. This room was much bigger and brighter than a sweat lodge, and I sensed everyone watching my every move. So, I closed my eyes and centered myself. As I opened my eyes, I began sensing the woman's energy sitting in the middle of the circle.

I sensed stuck anger in her belly by the way she was sitting. She was crying as Tati placed a rock on the back of her head. I approached her and gently modeled an "Ah" sound until she began doing it herself. Modeling the Ah a little louder, I supported her in gently amplifying the sound—it turned into a yell and then a scream. Monique motioned for me to take a bowl of the liquid tobacco and rub on the woman's belly. As I approached her, I whispered in her ear what I was going to do and asked if she could raise her blouse. I then began gently applying the tobacco on her belly and lower back in circular strokes, checking in with her with each application.

She began to relax and soften, and the session slowly came to a close. As I took my seat, Monique turned to me and said, "You did that so gently."

I replied, "I am a man, in front of thirty women, asking a woman to raise her blouse so I can touch her, as she is most likely processing an abuse. Treating her with respect was not only right; it was part of the healing."

At the end of the ceremony, Tati asked me to close the ceremony. I could barely remember what Monique had said when she called in the directions, but I closed my eyes and stood facing the East and just allowed spirit to guide my words as I beat the drum. Bear Claw, a shaman in attendance, sounded a resounding "aho," *amen,* so I knew my closing resonated.

My confidence was growing by jumping in head first, surrendering to the moment, allowing the guidance of spirit to speak through me. It felt messy for this Virgo, but I was being trained. Being invited to call the directions is a privilege that has deepened my understanding of their wisdom.

I thought of all of the other things I *could have done* on the flight home instead of acknowledging *what I did.* There was still a lot to learn when it came to loving myself.

When I returned home, my bed was empty without Greta. The next night, Oscar began to sleep next to me. His presence soothed my grief.

Connie had mentioned to me in a recent session that Greta had been training Oscar on how to take care of me. He learned well.

Divine Love

Mom was not well. As I gazed at her struggling to see the television or her computer screen, and witnessing how her friend's dying was weighing on her, my heart filled with compassion. I saw her vulnerability. We both recognized the impermanence of this physical life.

During the early stages of my spiritual journey, I had focused on separating myself from my parents as a vital aspect of my personal development. Reconnecting with my mother and assisting her in overcoming her debilitating pain and immobility has been transformative. When I accessed unconditional love and forgiveness in that first sacred medicine ceremony in Ecuador, it not only changed my life forever; it transformed my relationship with her.

After forty-some years of separation, I see, sense, and feel her deep love for me. She thanks me every day for helping her, and we are now close friends, helping each other as we share this special moment in time together.

Love is Divine. Love and light represent innate states of our existence. The Divine light surrounds us and flows through us.

Divine Light

Weaving the truth of my experiences with sacred medicine and ascension/ multi-dimensional beingness, I found that once Divine light arrives, it can no longer be denied.

This light restores each molecule of our beings to its highest state of optimal health. This essential healing life force within us is ever present. It animates us.

When I slow down, drop into my body, and allow myself to relax, I can sense it. The vital healing life force connects me with All That Is. As I open up to these greater levels of flow, every cell of my body is infused with the light of Spirit.

The medicine stays with us forever.

Subtle Bodies

In my next Integrated Beingness class, I reviewed the different energetic layers that comprise my aura or auric energy system. The most talked about are the etheric, emotional, mental, and spiritual layers—these energies form the luminous energy field.

Human beings are multidimensional, with subtle bodies that vibrate at different frequencies and interact energetically with both the physical and non-physical worlds.

As I learned from the shamans, flow and movement of subtle energy throughout the body can have major effects on your health and wellbeing. This is how shamans and those who study Reiki can heal someone's energetic or subtle body, and it affects their physical body.

These subtle bodies begin at the physical body and extend outwards. They correlate to the seven chakras, the spinning centers of energy located along your central channel, the inner core near the spine. The most commonly referred to are the seven chakras along your spine, but I learned there are many more above, below, and around the body.

Chakras

My studies of ascension light work, with Integrated Beingness, was deepening my connection to the field that surrounds me and my chakras. Each chakra is a spinning "wheel" of energy that correlates to various mental and physical qualities. Our chakras spin, but unresolved emotions and disempowering thoughts can unbalance them. Sensing and feeling when the chakras are in or out of balance is an important part of aligning with Source.

My solar plexus and sacral chakras are where I carried the deepest wounds and the greatest need for clearing—centers tied to my sexuality, creativity, and self-worth. Ayahuasca and ascension work have helped me heal my sacral and solar plexus, cleansing the pain and replacing it with divine light energy to love and reprogram my subconscious mind.

The most challenging lesson for me was that no one was coming to save me. As a boy I created strategies to get the support I craved. None of them worked. In the first half of my life, I focused on becoming what I needed to survive. I became everything for everyone, and I lost my soul. I didn't accept parts of my body. My organs and chakras began living their trauma, creating their own separate intentions, and I lived a life that didn't belong to me. I was a victim.

When I learned that ascension is actually the soul descending into the body, it clicked for me. The ascension process is not rising or leaving our bodies but the descent of spirit into matter—embodiment of the soul. That was what I had always intended to do.

Wounds Are Gifts

I asked for more guidance from an astrologer, and she pointed out how the asteroid Chiron was influencing my chart recently. Chiron is an archetype known as the Wounded Healer. He was an unwanted child who was abandoned at birth. Chiron symbolizes the profound wounds we carry into this life and those we accumulate along our journey. These enduring wounds seem to become woven into the very essence of who we are. Chiron guides us to embrace our wounds and channel them into gifts of healing, compassion, and intuition.

Connecting with the archetype of Chiron supported me in seeing my wounds as gifts. As Rumi[57] said, my wounds are where the light has entered me. Feeling unsafe taught me how to pay attention to subtle energies. The hypersensitivity I developed as a coping mechanism made me super attuned to people's energy. Because of my challenged vision, I first felt energy in others kinesthetically[58] instead of visually.

Connecting with Unseen Beings

Easily sensing people's energy, Lorna and Louise guided me deeper into the study of ascension and multidimensional and quantum[59] energy practices—and this newfound knowledge mirrored and enhanced my work with my Reiki master, Connie.

Now I was also seeing and sensing other energetic fields more clearly. It reminded me of the light Barry emanated and like galactic beings and the spirits I'd seen in Ecuador and Puerto Rico.

---

[57] Rumi was a 13th-century Persian poet, theologian, and Sufi mystic, widely recognized for his profound and spiritual poetry that explores themes of love, unity, and the divine.

[58] *Kinesthetically*: adverb describing the manner in which information is processed or learned through physical movement and bodily sensations. In educational and developmental contexts, kinesthetic learning involves engaging in hands-on activities and physical exercises to enhance understanding and retention. This learning style emphasizes the body's role in acquiring knowledge and skills, often benefiting those who are more responsive to experiential and tactile methods of engagement.

[59] In physics and metaphysics, the quantum field refers to the fundamental field that underlies all particles and forces in the universe, believed to be a source of infinite potential and interconnectedness. In spiritual contexts, the quantum field is often described as the underlying energetic reality from which consciousness and matter emerge, suggesting that individual thoughts and intentions can influence this field, thereby shaping experiences and realities through the principles of quantum mechanics.

With the support of Connie and Lorna, I connected with the spiritual realm of guides, archangels,[60] and ascended masters[61] that I had once disregarded, not believing in their existence. While studying archangels and ascended masters, I was astonished to recognize their images. Their faces I saw in books were the beings who had visited me in Puerto Rico: Archangels Uriel and Metatron and Ascended Master Vywamus. I began connecting with them and asking for their assistance.

Divine Wisdom – Asking for Help

When struggling to access unconditional love, I began to seek guidance from my spiritual guides and ascended masters. Initially, using Joshua David Stone's[62] phrase I read about in my cohort, "Please help me," felt disempowering, but directing it to Source and my guides proved effective. Within minutes, I felt my body soften, my breath deepen as I returned to peace and alignment. By connecting with figures like Quan Yin and Buddha, I remembered the importance of asking for help and receiving their wisdom.

Many of my experiences in Integrated Beingness resonated with the messages I received in ceremonies during my trips to Ecuador. For instance, in a class of Integrated Beingness, I learned gestures to align my hara[63] and

---

[60] *Archangels* are high-ranking angels in various religious traditions, believed to serve as messengers and protectors, often associated with specific roles, virtues, and domains within spiritual hierarchies.

[61] *Ascended masters* are enlightened beings who have transcended physical existence and are believed to guide and assist humanity in spiritual development, often recognized in New Age and esoteric teachings.

[62] Joshua David Stone was an author and spiritual teacher known for his writings on personal development, spirituality, and the integration of Eastern and Western philosophies.

[63] In Eastern traditions and various holistic practices, the *hara* refers to the energy center located in the lower abdomen, considered crucial for physical vitality and emotional stability. Often associated with the concept of groundedness, the hara is believed to be the source of life force energy (qi or chi) and plays a vital role in martial arts, meditation, and healing practices, serving as the foundation for balanced physical and spiritual well-being.

antakarana bridge,[64] which had synchronicity with the gesture that came through me in my first ceremony in Ecuador as I looked at the fire.

In our meditations, we were guided to sit on our throne of divinity and sovereignty to connect to our higher heart[65] and consciousness. This mirrored the throne I saw in my second ceremony in Ecuador. When I shared these synchronicities with Lorna, she said to me, "You are integrating Divine wisdom on deeper levels."

In October, I had another opportunity to join Tati and Monique to deepen and weave the knowledge I was gaining with Lorna. So I headed back to Syracuse. This ceremony was smaller and intimate. I was able to ask more questions. I asked Tati, "Why do you use rocks and feathers in cleansings and ceremonies?"

"Because," Tati said, "they are older than we are and have wisdom."

I learned that elements of nature hold a collective memory, and this memory is responsible for a telepathic connection among organisms. I began to believe we are being asked to rejoin this relationship that we abandoned and develop our telepathic, psychic, and clairvoyant abilities and sensing powers.

---

[64] A symbolic representation in metaphysical and spiritual teachings, the *Antakarana Bridge* refers to the pathway connecting the individual personality (lower self) with the higher aspects of consciousness (Higher Self or divine source). It is often described as a bridge of energy that facilitates communication and alignment between the conscious and subconscious mind, promoting spiritual development and integration of higher wisdom into daily life.

[65] A concept in spiritual and holistic practices representing an elevated state of emotional and spiritual consciousness, often associated with compassion, love, and unity. The *Higher Heart* is thought to transcend the traditional heart center, connecting individuals to deeper aspects of their being and facilitating greater empathy and understanding in relationships. It is viewed as a vital energy center for healing, self-awareness, and spiritual growth.

I watched Tati and Monique, seeing and sensing the same things that were out of balance with the participants, working with ease together. My mind began to question my sensing abilities when I joined them for a cleansing. I saw different imbalances and felt unsure if what I was seeing was true. Having two experiences of working with divination tools, I didn't trust my connection to them. Feelings of comparison and inadequacy regarding my own abilities rose.

The day after the ceremony, Monique, Tati and I hiked at Green Lakes State Park—two glacial lakes surrounded by upland forest. Monique developed Earth-based psychotherapy, which holds the premise that Mother Earth can transmute what we are ready to let go of. She teaches others a practice of placing pains and fears on an object from nature (for example, a rock) and offering it back to the earth for Mother Earth to transmute.

As I was still feeling this comparison that I wanted to let go of, I found a heavy rock and began carrying it. Monique noticed and said, "Why are you carrying that?"

I said, "There is something heavy I need to let go of. I'm doing what you teach."

"Oh, OK," she replied.

As I walked down to the lake, I imbued the deep-seated feeling of comparison from my solar plexus into the rock and asked the lake to take it from me. As I placed the rock into the lake, I gave thanks. This lightness filled my solar plexus and expanded through my body with each step back as I rejoined Monique and Tati.

Owning that and releasing the comparison, I knew it wasn't toward anyone, but rather a block to my sense of worth. This lightness continues. The lightness allowed me to completely marvel at and appreciate how beautiful Monique and Tati's dance of leading is to watch and receive. They had been dancing together for years, and I have different qualities that I would weave with Tati in our first dance together a few months later in Ecuador.

The next morning, Tati and I woke up at 3:00 a.m. I drove us to the airport to catch our flights home. We ate breakfast together, and I spoke to her about my process. She said to me, "The earth, rocks, animals, and the trees are always here, supporting you."

It was at that moment I realized that the deeper my connection to the earth, the more I found my soul's true home.

Connecting with My Ancestral Land

It was the last day of October. I'd just returned from the ceremony in New York.

Earlier in October, my British friend Barry asked me, "When can I meet you in the flesh?" Feeling uncertain about when to visit, I consulted my pendulum to find the ideal time, and it indicated December. This guidance left me perplexed, as I had a retreat scheduled in Costa Rica at that time.

Later that afternoon, I received a call informing me that the retreat in Costa Rica was cancelled. When I contacted Barry, he urged me, "Come!" Greater forces were at play.

My mother expressed her worries about me traveling to a foreign country to meet a man I had never encountered before. She had numerous fear-driven questions, yet deep down, I felt it was my destiny to meet Barry.

When I told my brother, he unearthed our Westwood family history in our mother's basement. To my surprise, our ancestors hailed from a region just minutes away from where Barry lived! This discovery transformed my visit into something much deeper—a remarkable ancestral journey filled with synchronicities. Everything unfolded as I set off on Thanksgiving Day.

Barry picked me up at London's Heathrow Airport. He approached me a bit frazzled. We hugged tightly for a minute, and he said, "Your energy is so calming. Thank you." It was like we had known each other all our lives—actually, we knew it was many lifetimes.

Still a bit frazzled, Barry couldn't find his car in the garage. When he finally located his White Range Rover, I sauntered to the wrong side of his car and tried to open the driver's side door, much to his amusement. It dawned on me that I was no longer in the United States.

On our way to the Midlands, Barry stopped at a market to pick up a chicken, for his roasted chicken dinner. He was serving me his specialty for my first night in England. I picked two over stuffed bouquets as a gift for his wife, Michelle.

As we resumed our journey, Barry disclosed the source of his discomfort: a business arrangement in which a partner had acted deceitfully, taking all the profits from a project they had collaborated on. He again expressed his gratitude for my calming presence. Barry made a turn into the English countryside. For the next hour, I sat in awe of the fairytale cottages nestled inside hedged roads—it was like driving through an endless mystical garden. I immediately felt a familiarity with the countryside of the Midlands that was cellular, deeper than I have felt in the United States.

It started to mist as we pulled up the driveway to his modern farm house. As Barry parked and unloaded my bags, he pointed to a lone oak tree in the field to our left. Its bare branches formed a mystical sphere. Barry said, "That tree is sacred." I would soon find out.

Ahead was a pre-fab rectangular box Barry had converted into a salon. The light was on, and I could barely make out the two women inside through the fogged windows. Michelle, his wife, was placing aluminum foil strips on a woman's head—dying her hair.

To my right, the lights from inside the house guided us through the mist. When Barry opened the front door, there lay Sol, an affectionate black tuxedo cat, and his sister, "Princess" Lua, a fluffy calico. Lua was aloof compared to Greta, so I approached her with respect and we warmed up quickly. I had brought a plush, multicolored, glow-in-the-dark unicorn blanket as a gift for Barry's five year old daughter, Sofia. Her voluminous black curls were a reflection of her Brazilian heritage from her mother. Sofia shyly nodded at me and jumped into her dad's arms, exclaiming "Dahty" in her cute British accent. Barry said, "This is 'Uncle Gregg,' and he has a present for you." Without hesitation, she unwrapped it swiftly, draping it over her shoulders and strutting around the house like Queen Elizabeth.

After the savory meal, I walked upstairs and collapsed from jet lag.

The next morning, Barry took me to Stratford-Upon-Avon. As we strolled through the ancient graves in the cemetery next to the church where Shakespeare is buried, I encountered a massive old tree. Its bark was gnarled and twisted, and its trunk was so wide. Its canopy sprawled, and the sheer scale evoked a sense of wonder and respect. I often venture into the forest to connect with the trees. First, I ask, "May I enter your space?" I approach, close my eyes, and place my hands on the tree and absorb the wisdom it imparts—receiving it through my hands.

This tree was so powerful; as I touched it, my entire body flooded with the brightest light. I heard encouraging words to be persistent. The tree seemed to know what I was going through. It reminded me that growth requires patience.

The next day we drove through the gorgeous Cotswolds on our way to Avebury. Barry hinted that the land there was powerful. I soon found out.

I had never seen so many shades of green, and this vibration from the ground entered into my feet and traveled throughout my limbs. My senses were on overload, but they were not overwhelming me or dysregulating my nervous system. Instead, I felt completely blissful. Barry and I began giggling in sheer delight and we couldn't stop as we ventured up a never-ending hill to visit a sacred temple.

Connecting to this earth was an ancestral healing. I sensed my ancestors had called me back to remember how to be in relationship with this magical earth. My ancestors were no longer imaginary. Walking on the mystical land of 6,000-year-old stone circles in Avebury, each stone imbued a sacred energy—they glowed. The stones had wise faces. I sensed their wisdom, like Tati had said. They were helping me remember the time when my ancestors were full of love, sacredness, and deep connection.

As we finally reached the top of the hill, Barry asked the spirits' permission to enter the sacred temple hidden inside the hill. Barry looked at me and nodded and we respectfully began to walk through the narrow stone entrance. I paused and kneeled and kissed the ground before entering. Carrying my drum, I entered the cold darkness. The stone beams reminded me of photos of Stonehenge. Barry sat down on the dirt floor, and I sat across from him. We sat in silence and sensed the sacredness. I began to beat my drum to honor the ancestors present. The vibration of my drum beats echoed through the chamber. A couple of tourists entered and left quickly. We sensed they knew not what we were doing.

One man, however, stayed for a while. He kneeled with us for several minutes.

As we left the temple, he was standing and greeted us with "Guh-day" in a thick Australian accent. Luke was a young man from Tasmania. Barry and I sensed he felt the same power we did in the temple by the way he gazed at us. A reverence he wasn't quite clear about.

Luke stayed as Barry and I meandered down the hill. As night fell, we slowly navigated our way back to the local pub in pitch darkness. As we entered the pub, there was Luke, standing at the bar, and we asked him to join us. We had a lovely heart-centered chat. Luke shared about his time in the military. He had seen many horrific acts, and his body was beaten from war injuries, and yet he was grateful for being alive.

Barry and I treated Luke to Shepard's pie and a draft. These seemingly random connections make life so special. Souls finding each other to share and learn about the mystery of this life together. Thoroughly enriched from the magical day, we returned to Barry's home.

This was the night before our outing to the town where my great-great-great-grandparents wed in 1798. I still wasn't sure which church was the right one. As I searched through the churches of the town, I found one with a directory of marriages dating back centuries—Saint Mary's of Kidderminster. There they were—William Westwood and Jane Clark.

In the morning, Barry and I collected Lorna from the local train station. Along with the excitement of finally meeting Barry, I was eager to connect with Lorna. She had done extensive research on my family tree. However, upon reaching the church, we discovered that it was locked. Feeling disappointed, Barry was resolute about getting us inside, so he circled the church, trying every door. Having no luck, the three of us took a moment and closed our eyes to express our intention to enter.

Within minutes, a car pulled up, and a tall, thin man popped out and said, "Hello. I am Alan, the caretaker. How may I assist you?" He offered to take us on a private tour. As we followed Alan through the rooms, he shared the church's history and the meanings behind the gorgeous stained-glass windows. When we reached the sanctuary, I stood in silence, imagining what my grandparents looked like and how they felt the day they married.

After our special tour, the three of us commented on how we sensed many spirits in the walls of the beautiful church, as we drove to a lovely market square. We meandered through Christmas trees, fresh produce, herbs, and homemade crafts, absorbing the scents of the holidays until we arrived at the cafe.

As we conversed over a proper English breakfast, Lorna asked, "If you had a T-shirt that said who you were on it, what would it say?" She claimed the Convenor, Barry, was the Navigator and me the Integrator. These were our Source-given talents, the driving forces of our souls' blueprints[66] to be of service to Source and humanity. Together we sensed we were to co-create something together.

Afterward, we headed back to Barry's house for some plum bread and tea. Dilraj, or Dil as he is fondly called, came to join us. His jet-black hair, deep brown skin, and gentle eyes felt oddly familiar. Dil's voice carries an angelic quality, a sweetness that resonated deeply within me. This was the first time we had met in the flesh. As we embraced, he pulled back and said, "I know I have met you before—just not in this lifetime." I nodded in agreement.

Sipping our tea, we started talking about podcasts, and both Lorna and I said we had wanted to host one but didn't know how. Dil helps others in creating podcasts. We all agreed, "Let's do one together!" So we began the process of creating our podcast, now named *Our Souls Speak*. Little did we know the unforeseen magic in store for us.

My trip ended with a weekend alone in London. It was Christmas time, and nowhere does Christmas better than London. The lights and store windows were spectacular. Everything was perfect—except for the weather.

---

[66] A *soul blueprint* is a metaphysical concept suggesting that each individual has a unique energetic plan or purpose that guides their life experiences and spiritual evolution. See Linda Backman, *Soul Evolution: Past Lives and Present Miracles* (Charlottesville, VA: Rainbow Ridge Books, 2014).

With my umbrella attempting to protect me, I braved the strong currents of wind and cold, driving rain. Walking around aimlessly, I remembered my friend Noor had asked me to bring her a box of chocolates from Harrods, the famous department store. A bit lost, I started to think I'd never find it, but as I turned a corner, there stood Harrods. I continued through Hyde Park and by Kensington Palace on my way to Portobello Market in Notting Hill, a bohemian neighborhood Barry thought I would like. I ducked out of the rain into this beautiful shop of ancient stones and earthy textiles. The store cleared out as I perused. I found an incense stone I liked and carried it to the desk, complimenting the owner, Katrina, on how beautiful her store was.

In a gravelly, deep British accent. "You're the most interesting person to grace my store all day!" As we continued our conversation she asked, "What is your name?" I told her, and she gasped, "I have Westwood in my lineage." One might think Westwood is a common last name, but it isn't.

Katrina shared that we were metal workers. *Grandpa Joe and "Daddy Joe," his father, owned a foundry in Kansas City.* The threads were weaving. And before that, we were gypsies. There are many misconceptions about gypsies—they were actually so clean they survived the Black Death, which killed almost half of the population of England in the 1300s. A couple of people entered the store, so as our conversation came to a close, I asked her if she could recommend a restaurant for a bite to eat and a drink. Katrina suggested the restaurant next door as I left, and after an appetizer, I hailed a black cab in the rain and went back to my hotel.

Arriving at my room, I collapsed on my bed, exhausted, and relived every moment of my truly magical trip in mysterious England.

Rest and Integration

When I returned to the US, I was not the same, and my body needed to rest to integrate the slew of experiences I'd had over the past year. Thankfully, the bitter cold December and January weather supported me in resting.

I needed to retreat inward to breathe life into this book. It was painful revisiting my traumas, my secrets. *Do I even want them to be seen?* The fear of being judged returned. Revisiting my past in the very home where many of those experiences took place was difficult, and I found it challenging to shape my expansive experiences into a cohesive form.

Recognizing the need for rest involved listening to my body before it demanded attention. Slowing down revealed that my way of showing love was exhausting, prioritizing others over myself. Through rest, I learned that love can be effortless and radiant, without leading to depletion. In a society that rewards burnout, I now prioritized my own needs, realizing that self-love wasn't solely based on what I give.

My body and nervous system needed rest to integrate my experiences and heightened sensitivity. During this time, I disconnected to help my cells assimilate. By embracing unconditional self-love, I've changed how I share love, focusing on nurturing myself first, allowing me to radiate love without exhaustion.

State of Being

After the holidays and resting, I was no longer the person I used to be. My energy field configurations had shifted. My new vibration surpassed my former state of existence, and my state of being became my priority.

Prioritizing my state of being; living in love, light, and power is not a mere wish—it is a daily commitment for me. This ongoing practice transformed how I approach life.

Over the past few years, I discovered that my state of being—what I hold sovereignty over—is sacred. I alone choose what I think, say, and do. By attuning to my body and subtle bodies, I've learned to discern my true state of being and to recognize which thoughts and feelings are truly mine.

Incorporating indigenous and multidimensional wisdom, I learned how crucial it was to safeguard not only my physical body but also my subtle bodies from unwanted energies.

Protection, Opening and Purification

I learned from Connie and Lorna the significance of forming a golden spiral or pillar of light as a shield of energetic protection. I invoke my spirit team of archangels and ascended masters to safeguard me, my home, my loved ones, and my travels. This protective space allows the armor of the body and heart to soften, fostering a sense of safety that encourages my body to open, expand, and receive more Source energy.

My cohort had supported me in a dynamic process of clearing and opening my body, creating more space for this vibrant energy while addressing what still needed to be released.

My somatic journey had been a long one, peeling away the armor that once shielded me. I shed all that the world imposed to dim my light. Purification entails a profound cleansing and release of numerous layers of both the physical and subtle bodies. This energetic cleansing mirrors the insights gained from ayahuasca.

I utilize breath, water, fire, and herbs in my daily cleansing practices to transmute what I am ready to let go of. More profound issues may require me to partake in ceremonies or breathwork sessions for deeper cleansing. There I utilize medicine, expression, and movement to release this stagnant energy so I can allow the life force to flow freely again. As I cleared my body and psyche, I created more space to receive the Divine.

Shortly after my soul merged, descended into my body, and I integrated this transformation, I no longer looked above for my connection to Source. My spiritual support team transitioned from above my head to around my body, now at eye level and accessible. My consciousness had rooted in the fifth dimension.

Through my practice remaining clear I attained higher levels of consciousness. Weaving my somatic practices, indigenous learnings, and multidimensional wisdom supported my intention to live in unconditional love.

With the power of unconditional love—by embodying my soul—I show up differently. I perceive life in a new light. Everything becomes more vibrant and alive in its energy, and I can navigate the world from a fresh perspective. This new setpoint is who I am. My new vibration was offering me opportunities to create new pathways that are aligned with its frequency. This alignment was being supported by my friends in the UK.

In February, Lorna, Barry and I, along with our friend Dil, began recording the *Our Souls Speak* podcast. One of our intentions was to share with the world how we, along with others, live each day from the frequency of unconditional love—our true essence. We aimed to listen, share, and discover how our souls communicate in harmony and unity-embodying Oneness.

My Integration

At the same time, this theme of harmony was woven into the retreat Tati and I were making the final preparations for. It was a month before our retreat when I held the pre-retreat call for the participants to prepare them for their week-long journey in Ecuador—the culture, what they should bring, and to remind them to set their intentions for the retreat. This was our first meeting—the first time we would see each other before meeting face-to-face in a part of the world they were unfamiliar with. I sensed their trepidation and excitement.

The meeting was surreal for me. *This is really happening!* I thought. *The Embodied Heart Retreat: Weaving the Divine Feminine and Masculine Energies to Activate the Power to Create* represented the creative culmination of two years spent integrating my journeys to Ecuador with the multidimensional embodiment of my soul's ascension. It was the action step—the manifestation of my vision.

Source had showed me a round room with four large open doors revealing beautiful trees. People were sitting in a circle, and I was leading movement and breath experiences. I had seen photos of the location where we were holding the retreat, but I would soon be surprised by what Source had in store for us.

My first trip to Ecuador connected me to the Divine Feminine energy of Grandmother. On my second trip, I was initiated into the Divine Masculine. On my third visit, I experienced oneness by connecting to my spiritual support team and began weaving the two Divine energies in my heart. What happened at the Embodied Heart retreat on my fourth visit was so transformative. I am not the same.

....

"In shamanic cultures, synchronicities are
recognized as signs you are on the right path."
—Daniel Pinchbeck

....

11

The Me Turns into WE

I flew overnight with three connections to Guayaquil, Ecuador's biggest city on the coast. Arriving in a soft rain, palm trees greeted me. The hot and humid weather was unlike the dry and temperate, mountainous Quito. Christian, a short round man who smiled all the time, greeted me and took me to his pickup truck. He didn't speak much English, but my Spanish had improved, so we had a basic conversation over the half hour down the highway.

Christian made a right turn, and we entered a dirt road for the rest of our hour drive into the lush mountains. The road was treacherous; we bounced up and down over holes in the dirt.

I was the first to arrive at Inkary, an eco retreat center. Christian took my bag to my suite on the top floor. The view from the suite was stunning. The birds greeted me, and I unpacked a bit and laid on the bed to rest from my long journey.

At 3:00 p.m., the loudest thunderclap I ever heard jolted me out of my light sleep. It felt like an omen—a message from the sky spirits. I sensed this was going to be a powerful retreat.

In the morning, I wandered the hilly terrain, crossing paths with ducks and a pack of wild horses. Yellow, orange, and blue butterflies rose from the road, fluttering beside me with each step.

Weaving the Divine Feminine and Masculine Energies to Activate the Power to Create

The other participants arrived and gathered over the next few days, some from the US and some from Ecuador. Tati and her crew arrived the next afternoon, and we connected briefly about the retreat. She was impressed with my improved Spanish.

On the first day, Tati prepared an offering for the land. As we planted it under a tree outside the temple, we greeted the spirits there and asked permission to do our work. We then held Family Constellations, and everyone's hearts became open and exposed. The next day, we finished the constellations before our sweat lodge. I drummed the whole ceremony and continued to deepen my relationship with my drum. The following day, I led a breathwork session. Tati joined as a first-time participant and was a little scared. After the session, everyone thanked me for my voice, as they said its strength held them through their deep release. I supported each in finding a gesture for their experience and to offer the movement to fire burning in the center.

The shaman for the ayahuasca ceremony, a French man who had lived in India before spending twenty years in Brazil with his teacher, arrived later that afternoon and met with all of the first-time participants.

The next morning, we rested before our ceremony with Grandmother. As I entered the temple, I chose the seat beside the shaman. For this ceremony, the altar was the fire in the center adorned with fresh flowers and crystals. The shaman hand delivered the first cup of ayahuasca to each of us. As he sang for the entire first round, I hummed and sang softly. I still don't comprehend fully how I know the melodies—they are etched in my cells, I think.

After he stopped singing, he revealed that this was the cleansing round. As I gazed into the flickering flames, I centered my thoughts on the purpose of our Embodied Heart retreat—weaving the Divine Feminine and Masculine energies to activate the power to create. I prayed for clarity on what I needed to release, both for myself and for the group I was guiding. After drinking the second cup of the ceremony, I closed my eyes and sank into my body. What I needed to let go of was far greater than just myself and those gathered around the fire.

The Cycle Breaker

The shaman started singing praises of Kali—the fierce and powerful goddess of destruction, the Divine Mother, protector of the innocent and bestower of enlightenment. Her energy simmered within my belly, swelling and growing stronger with every song, until it erupted in waves, flowing through my fingertips and toes like a river.

I was releasing the toxic masculine energy stored within my cells and DNA. Looking up, I encountered my ancestors, whom I had kept at arm's length because of their judgments, racism, and the effects of their colonization. They pleaded with me for forgiveness. Grandmother embraced me once more, and in that moment, I could forgive them effortlessly. Turning back to the fire, a radiant stream of light flowed into my belly, filling the void with a force. It was the essence of the Divine Masculine. An electric vibration filled my body followed by an exalted realization that changed the context of my life.

Embodying this presence, I no longer needed to perform to be loved and respected. Its power was Beingness.

The Divine Feminine power of Kali liberated the toxic masculine energy within me. The Divine Feminine energy of Grandmother Ayahuasca held me, instilling in me the compassion to forgive, opening my heart to allow the Divine Masculine to flow in and expand into every cell. The Divine Feminine and Masculine weaving together activated a power within me I had not sensed before. The best way I can describe the sensation was a beam of radiance. Inherent in that beam was a knowing—a knowing of safety that supports my inner child. He is now safe to create, play, and feel the joy he lost.

I had experienced the intention of our retreat. One unexpected gift of receiving the Divine Masculine energy was a sense of lightness. By embracing Divine power, I could experience Divine Light. Everyone around me noticed the shift in my consciousness, embodiment, and vibration. Tati hugged me and wept. "Oh, Gregorio, your hug is so healing," she said. "I needed this divine masculine energy to feel safe enough to feel my Divine Feminine." For me, it was effortless—a radiant presence larger than myself that I felt compelled to share simply by being it. My authenticity and coherence modelled what I had attempted to preach before. I radiated this support to others, now not needing anything in return.

After the ceremony, one of the male participants confided in me; he felt afraid when I got up and walked around during the event. He feared he couldn't endure the challenges he was facing in the ceremony without my strength beside him. I listened, feeling both disbelief and joy. No man had ever conveyed they desired to be supported by my strength.

Healing alongside the group members while leading—helping others awaken while staying rooted in humility—was profound. My healing was our healing.

Interconnectedness

The ceremony's blessings lingered even after I departed the temple. Upon returning to my room at 3:00 a.m., my thoughts were broken by several loud 'neighs.' Looking out the window, I spotted the magnificent stallion from the wild herd that roamed the land. He continued to call out, and as I expressed my gratitude, he galloped away into the moonlit darkness.

In South America, every interaction with nature is a communication, and it was clear to me that the stallion was acknowledging, if not celebrating, my transformation.

Animals are messengers. When we embody our soul and radiate who we truly are, animals feel it, the earth feels it, and they celebrate with us—this is the interconnection with all life.

Embracing and embodying the Divine Masculine energy had been the missing piece in my life for a long time. By shielding my inner child from my ancestors, particularly my grandfathers, I was rejecting their gifts and assistance. Instead of letting them nurture me, I remained trapped in my wounds and anger. Forgiveness is a gift, liberating me from the victimhood that controlled me. Although I was perceived as masculine, it was a mask, hiding my vulnerability and sexuality—one I began wearing in junior high.

By integrating this transformative energy, I realized I allowed my wounded inner child to shape a familiar world. Throughout much of my life, I remained a boy in my relationships and with Source, hoping for, searching for, and chasing an energy I felt undeserving of. With a key root of my inner critic healed, the light of the fire healed my solar plexus and sacrum where the wounds of my childhood lived. My wounded child had been unconsciously living life through me.

On this trip, I forgave them all.

Order returns when we retrieve our fragmented pieces from abuse that caused the wound, discerning what is ours and what is not. Then balance and harmony are restored, and only love remains.

The next day, on our integration hike, Tati put us in a specific order. We were instructed to stay in our designated place at all times and not speak. She was supporting the return to order from the pains in each person's life that were revealed and healed during the retreat. After a deep release, it is important to return to alignment and open to receive the flow of Source or life energy into our bodies to fill the spaces, as the stream from the fire of Divine Masculine energy had filled me in the ceremony.

The embodiment of the Divine Masculine energy was enhanced by connecting to the sacred medicine equivalent in San Pedro during our integration trek to the waterfall the next day. The slippery, steep hike was effortless for me this time, unlike the struggle I'd experienced two years ago. As I aligned with the energy, it fueled and protected me. *Older, yet stronger. How is that possible?* The life force had filled me with power and was integrating deeper into my cells with each step.

My embodiment of the Divine Masculine energy gave me a fresh sense of my power and the realization of my unique contribution to my brotherhood. Once lacking the confidence to join other men in any public forum, because of my history of being bullied, I now feel inspired to sit with my brothers and contribute to the healing we all long for.

Our culture has been overrun with the negative aspects of masculinity, and so many of us want to erase masculinity and honor only the feminine. Having prided myself in being a safe man for women, I chose the feminine over the masculine to lead with. I often heard I had a gentle strength.

By embodying the Divine Masculine, I felt held by something bigger than me. My gentle strength was enhanced by a protective, empowered compassion. One of certainty in service to the whole—driven not by the aim to heal others but by a desire to serve Source and a readiness to help others.

Weaving these energies, the Divine Masculine now has the support of the Divine Feminine, allowing me to receive. Yet another healing from my first hike.

During the closing circle, I found myself in tears as I expressed to the group how they, along with the temple, brought my vision to life, enriching my experience beyond what I could have envisioned. When I first arrived at the temple, it exceeded every expectation I had. The individuals who joined us were truly committed to exploring profound depths. Because we asked permission from the spirits of the land, because we honored the sky, the trees, and animals, they in turn supported our deep healing journey. I believe this magic unfolded because I set an intention and took Source-guided actions while surrendering the outcome to Source/Great Spirit.

Tati had not led a retreat in the same place for a week until this one, and after the participants left, we spoke of how deep we all went, especially us, the leaders. We were delighted at the opportunity to do it again. The owner of Inkary, Xavier, who had participated in our retreat, drove us to the airport and said he hoped we would return.

As I boarded my flight back to St Louis, I felt so much gratitude for this creation, its power and how Tati had supported me in developing—*retrieving*—my strength and leadership in such a short amount of time.

Mom instantly recognized a change in me when I arrived for a short visit before I was heading back to the UK in April. "You have a confidence I haven't seen before," she said. "You seem peaceful." My daily walks with Oscar in nature grounded this Divine energy I had received deeper into my cells with each step.

During the virtual integration sessions I conducted with each participant the next week, I witnessed their incredible transformations. The intensity of the sparkle in their eyes and the compassionate strength in their voices reflected their newfound, fierce, unconditional love, along with the stories they shared about the meaningful steps they were taking in their lives. In those moments, I experienced profound joy, knowing I was serving Source.

I only had another week to pack and get ready for my next adventure in the UK with Barry.

When he picked me up at the airport, Barry said, "Wow! Ecuador changed you, brother! I can feel it!" He noticed, too.

It was close to Easter, so I had brought Sophia a stuffed bunny. She squeezed it and carried it everywhere. Sol and Lua greeted me as if I hadn't left. I was home. Lorna arrived the next morning, as we were recording two live podcasts with guests from the UK.

After we recorded two live podcasts in Barry's living room, Lorna and I went outside to soak up the spring sun. I shared about my recent trip, and she commented on the shift she was witnessing in me—the Divine Masculine power. She noticed, too. Our discussion deepened, and we reflected on how retreats often conclude too soon. The joy and light arrive at the end, leaving many to navigate integration alone. While healing is vital, so is joy; we need to balance both.

Lorna paused and said her usual, "They are telling me..."—her way of signaling that her guides were speaking. Then she smiled and said, "Wouldn't it be wonderful to host a live event featuring our presenters?"

When Barry joined us to hear that statement, the three of us beamed and exclaimed in unison, "Yes!" We began sharing a vision of a different type of gathering with our podcast presenters. Maybe gathering in a field somewhere with fifty people. Little did we realize how this guidance from Source would evolve.

This was the beginning of an event that we would co-create in service to the earth, humanity and Source.

The next night, Barry and I had some time alone together, so we sat on the lounge chairs in his yard near this sacred oak tree. We carried the intention to create a sacred evening—one which would deepen our connection and shared vision for humanity. A connection that rooted my soul.

"When we heal something in ourselves it creates a flow back into time. It sends a healing impulse to our ancestors. And it sends a healing impulse to our culture."
—Thomas Hübl

12

Rooted Soul

It was the strawberry full moon. The sky was a dark blue, and four twinkling stars aligned in an angle extending down from the colossal pink moon. Her light guided us through the night.

We created an altar of crystals we brought and rocks and feathers I had gathered from our walk earlier that morning. I brought my drum and called in the directions, this time the Celtic versions, as I intended to honor the land. Barry brought his Viking ship talisman—his mother is Norwegian. We desired to honor our ancestors.

As we shared, we saw the same road ahead. At one point, Barry said, "I have your back." I felt my feet send roots deep into my ancestral land. No one had ever said that to me before. This commitment created a pact of sacred brotherhood.

Like many of my close relationships, I usher Barry to the earth, and he stretches me to the ethers. We both see the highest potential in everyone. I have felt disappointment when the people close to me were not embodying their potential, attached to their wounds, and yet it was because I was as well. When my inner state shifted—when I stopped trying to fix and heal the world—people treated me differently. The world is a mirror. It became clear Barry was different from my past connections. The difference was part Barry, part the shifts I had made.

Then Barry wanted to visit his sacred oak tree. Barefoot, he held onto my shoulders for the walk through the dry tilled farmland to the tree. Barry wobbled several times in pain as his bare feet scraped across the hard soil. Each step I took was steady and precise to support him. I had his back, too. When we arrived, the moon was at her peak, and we basked in her healing light. After relishing in the beauty of the earth and sky, we mindfully walked back toward our chairs and lay on the grass and star gazed. We lay there for several minutes, and Sol, Barry's cat, joined us and lay down between us.

With Barry, there was not an "I don't think I can do that" like I received from Tom or silence like I got from Daniel in response to my request for deep intimate conversations and connection in the past. Instead, I was met with "I'm all in." This willingness to go to the depths of our souls was what I had always wanted in my intimate relationships. I needed to stand in Divine power in order to receive. Barry was not only mirroring me; he was wanting more too. The depth of our connection serves as a blueprint for what is possible in my future intimate relationships.

It was time to go to sleep. As I turned toward Barry's house, I saw this beaming fence-like multidimensional framework with tiny lights glowing in every color. It was unyielding and translucent at the same time. I thought I was hallucinating from looking at the stars. Then I remembered Lorna told me she installed an energetic grid around Barry's house for protection. *It's actually real!* Any previous doubt dissolved. I approached the grid like I would a tree and asked permission to proceed through. As I proceeded and passed through on my way to Barry's house, I sensed any unwanted energy I may have picked up outside was cleansed. When we got inside, we both smiled and giggled while sipping the delicious broccoli and Stinton cheese soup he prepared us.

In the morning, Sofia woke me up in her adorable British accent, "Oncle Grahwgg, wake up please." It was going to be a great day. Barry had scheduled an acupuncture session with his friend Carolyn, whom we had interviewed for the podcast a couple of days before.

Carolyn greeted us with a kind smile. I discovered that beneath her curly red hair, fair skin, and angelic voice lay a powerful magician. She showed me to the treatment room, and I was drawn to a powerful wooden mask. Carolyn handed it to me, and tears streamed down my face as my heart quivered. I sensed the masculine energy that I was integrating and felt vulnerable. She held my hands, and I shared about my experience in Ecuador. Carolyn placed her hand on my chest, and the tears turned into sobbing. She sensed some energy in my sacrum, and I remembered that is where my snake guide resides.

Carolyn gently guided me to allow my snake to travel slowly up my spine, eventually reaching my crown chakra. My snake's presence in the space weaved around the Divine Masculine energy as a protective skin, which anchored that beam of energy I received in Ecuador. I had thought the snake's place was in my sacrum, but allowing him to inhabit my entire central channel became a resource I still use when I feel uncertain or fearful—another way I align.

Carolyn's power and her ability to be with mine pleasantly surprised me. I gave Carolyn a grateful embrace as she left me to lay on her table for several minutes to breathe with my tears.

After my powerful session, Barry and I headed south to the coast for a sound bath that evening. Sound is a creative force in the universe. This bath was less soothing than I was used to. The amplitude of the waves vibrated my tired body. But the frequency was healing, nonetheless. Healing sound frequencies harmonize my energy field, restoring balance within my body and mind. The sound flowed into my fingertips and toes, further deepening my embodied integration of the Divine Masculine energy.

The next morning, we journeyed to magical Glastonbury, considered the heart of Mother Earth. Barry, the Navigator, receives spontaneous guidance; he senses where we are to go next. Barry's sensing is deeper than an intuitive or sixth sense; he is shown the place visually in his mediation and connects to the field of awareness. I never know where we are going until right before we leave, and we always have a miraculous time on our journeys together.

As Barry made a right turn on the country road, there it was—the sacred Tor. On top of this sacred hill stands a roofless tower. Its simple presence is so ancient and powerful—I couldn't help but envision a time long ago. Arriving in the lively, spiritual town, we parked and walked to the base of the Tor where we met Barry's dear friend Jane. She carried her drum and led us in a short ceremony connecting to our hearts before we entered the White Spring.[67]

The iron gate swung open, and the flickering flames of twenty some candles thoughtfully placed on stone pedestals were the only light guiding us into this dark sacred cavern. The rising steam from the frigid spring cast a mystical wave pointing us to the Divine Feminine and Masculine altars to each side.

Barry and I sat on the stone ledge of the spring, mindfully setting our intentions for opening our hearts. I stepped in first, slowly lowering my body to be cleansed. The ice-cold water was my first cold cleanse. It was not easy to release, as my body hardened first from the frigid water. I had to focus. I received strength and alignment by staring straight into a

---

[67] The *White Spring in Glastonbury* is a natural spring located at the foot of Glastonbury Tor in Somerset, England, revered as a sacred site associated with pilgrimage, goddess traditions, and contemporary spiritual practices. See Marion Bowman, "Glastonbury: A New Age Pilgrimage Centre," *Religion* 19, no. 2 (April 1989): 117–132.

flickering candle flame. As I allowed myself to merge with the water, my heart cracked open, and I sensed cubes of ice dropping as they melted into the water.

My mind was frozen, as well. I released the remaining unconscious blocks to my heart through my frosty exhales. Feeling the support of the water and earth allows my heart to open—allows me to let go of all my contractions and holding—peeling away the layers that block my heart. I realize that my heart is made to break—its purpose is to burst open again and again so that it can hold ever more wonders.

Feeling complete—clean—I climbed out of the spring and walked toward my towel. Barry was sitting on the wooden bench where our belongings lay—I had lost track of his whereabouts with my focused mission—and he whispered to me, "You went into the spring so easily!"

As we dried off, I entered the Divine Masculine altar through an arch of branches. There were inspirational phrases etched in the stone, and the main statue on the altar was a man with antlers, sitting in the lotus position. He touched his heart, eyes closed, and he wore a soft smile. His presence reminded me of compassionate strength, and I felt blessed by his energy.

Barry was about to leave without entering the altar, so I motioned to him to join me. As I whispered, "You have to see this," I noticed he was crying. He laid his head on my shoulder as I wrapped my arm around his waist firmly. Barry had connected with his father, who was killed in combat when he was young. I felt so much compassion for him. We are not meant to do this alone.

My relationship with Barry has not only been adventurous; it has healed the pain, for both of us, of us not having unconditional love from other men. As I said, Barry and I compliment each other and we are both very connected to our bodies. He was a champion cyclist. Spiritually, we honor the body as a sacred vessel, one aligned to heaven and earth.

Barry's work is the Art of Possibility. Barry connects more with Father Sky's gifts of light, the Pleiadeans,[68] and unlimited possibility. He inspires me to expand my awareness. He sees shapes and colors; I see the energy of the land and living beings.

By connecting to the earth through my roots, I receive her nurturing energy. It flows into my feet and rises through my body. The act of grounding relaxes my body and mind—I can sense that I am supported. The more I let go into the earth, the more I am supported. Grounded, rooted in trust, my body softens and opens to receive the light from Source. These energies weave in my heart, and as I breathe deeply, they expand. My rooted soul then radiates love.

Many spiritual teachers make statements like, "I am not my body," or "This body is not me." Continuing to practice absorbing luminous energy and embodying its radiant vibration into our bodies, Barry and I both feel the responsibility to anchor the light to earth. Embodying love and light isn't sugary. It is not ignoring what is. Everything in the world is not OK. By weaving Divine power with love and light, our embodiment has bravery.

After our sacred time in Glastonbury, we drove to Barry's mum's house on the coast and spent the night with her. The next morning, I caught my flight back to the US.

....

"Love is the intended expression of all life forms."
—Joshua David Stone

....

---

[68] The *Pleiadeans* are described in New Age and channeling literature as an advanced extraterrestrial race from the Pleiades star cluster, believed to communicate spiritual wisdom and guidance to humanity. See Barbara Marciniak, *Bringers of the Dawn: Teachings from the Pleiadeans* (Bear & Company, 1992).

13

Trusting the Unfolding

After the long transatlantic flight and the two-hour shuttle ride, I arrived at Mom's house at midnight. As I opened the front door, I was joyfully greeted by sweet Oscar—a toy in his mouth and wagging his tail so hard it banged the door.

Oscar – Joy

Oscar greets everyone this way, and in that greeting is his gift of joy.

On our daily walks, he teaches me to meet each new day freshly as he bounds with elation and senses the earth and other living beings with wonder.

The morning after my return, on our walk, I was struggling with jet lag. An ice cream truck drove by, playing its cheerful tunes. Tilting his head back and forth, Oscar reminded me of the wonder and innocence of my inner child and its remarkable ability to rejuvenate my joy. His beingness sparked glee throughout my body.

I love him so much.

After resting for a few days, Mom and I noticed Oscar began looking up at the ceiling. This occurred every night for a week. The night of my monthly session with Connie, he sat on the bed next to my desk at attention. Oscar seemed very concerned. I told Connie, "It looks like he sees something." I paused and then shared, "You know, this was the room where my father passed."

She asked, "Did Oscar know your father?"

I said, "No."

Connie said, "Let's ask your dad what he wants." As I lay next to Oscar for our session, I sensed Dad. He was concerned about Mom and offered his assistance in supporting her in her fear of dying. "Just tell her I'm OK," he said.

I said, "I will!" and sensed his energy moving away. Immediately, Oscar laid down and rested his head on my arm.

After our session, I went downstairs and told Mom. Simply telling Mom about that experience soothed her. She was reminded of when Oscar acted out, tearing up things, a few days before her dog Miata died suddenly. She said, "Oscar knows things."

The next morning, I rejoined my daily practice of opening, receiving, clearing and aligning my body to Source, rooted to the earth. I continued to weave my experiences into this book.

When I first started writing this book, I felt as though I had little wisdom to offer, much like my father's belief that he could never do enough. Reliving and then revealing my wounds to the world has been gut wrenching at times. I've avoided facing them, I've procrastinated, but I never gave up. My mind wanted the process to hurry up.

Change is messy at times, hard for this Virgo with a Libra rising. And I feel impatience with my Aries moon: *Let's do this NOW. Are we there yet?* There is no there. There is only the present moment.

I spent time judging the length of time my transition back to service took. *Did I waste those twenty years at the condominiums?* Every new experience needs time to integrate fully.

The Path Forward: Snake and Spirals

While the goal of the spiritual path is continual expansion, it is not about chasing expansive experiences beyond what I have the capacity to integrate. Through the process of integration, fear of the unknown nudges me towards the next level of unconditional self-love, establishing a new baseline energetic setpoint. My path is ongoing and continuous. It requires both discipline and patience. As I continued to write this book, I still wasn't certain what direction I was heading in.

I was reminded of what Tati said as I left New York.

The journey ahead is not a straightforward one; it resembles the movement of a snake, twisting and oscillating side to side, as well as moving backward and forward. Integration, much like healing, is non-linear. What once seemed healed resurfaced, prompting me to confront the same fears and lessons again, but at a more profound and often more painful level.

At first, I felt like I was regressing. Having released so much, I thought, *Didn't I already heal that? Why do I have to go there again?* As I went deeper, I sensed the spiraling energy I had experienced in my first Grandmother ceremony.

I've long been attracted to the transformational energy of the spiral and the power of its symbolism. Because the spiral represents our journey of going to the depths to transcend, I chose it as the logo for my company, Depth Integration.

I gained inspiration with the Spiral card from the *Mystical Shaman Oracle* deck.[69] Trusting the medicine of the spiral guides your journey of renewal. Surrendering to this journey until the exhausted paradigm dissolves into the depths of the psyche and its energy is released gives birth to a new reality.

I created a spiral with my crystals and feathers and entered the center slowly, intending to release to the earth what no longer served me. As I walked back out of the spiral, the same way I entered, I felt recharged to trust the unfolding of my new journey.

Standing in that trust, I realized I could stay stuck in wanting life to be the way I wanted it to be, or I could surrender to the magical unfolding of life and embrace the life that was trying to work its way into my consciousness. I wasn't just receiving divine qualities and energies—I was becoming them. I felt a deep sense of gratitude for all that was beginning to take form—the podcast, the event, this book.

The unknown was transforming from something to fear into a beautiful, magical adventure. As I continued, my visions and intentions began manifesting before my eyes, in ways more wondrous than I could have created alone, with effortless ease and grace. Yet they were never truly all "mine."

---

[69] The *Mystical Shaman Oracle Deck* is card deck, developed by Alberto Villoldo, for divination and spiritual guidance, featuring imagery and themes related to shamanic practices, mysticism, and healing. Designed to facilitate intuitive insights and personal reflection, the deck incorporates elements of nature, spirituality, and mythology, aimed at connecting users to their inner wisdom and the universal energy.

14

Service to the Divine

Everyone who knows me knows how deeply I love animals. I am grateful for my animal angels, Harry, Greta, and Oscar, who have taught me unconditional love and supported me through the phases of my life. By my side through the ups and downs, the power of their presence teaches me to love, to sense, hear, and see more deeply; to play and experience the magic of life through their innocence and childlike curiosity. I was always amazed when I'd consciously approach Harry and Greta's energy fields. They sensed me long before I touched them.

Animals are more attuned to subtle bodies and energy.

With their ability to sense more, their awareness of unseen energies and beings, they have supported me in honing my psychic abilities like clairvoyance, ESP, and telepathy. Animals show me what is possible. Their gifts inspire and motivate me to extend what I believe is possible to sense, see, hear, feel and know.

So, the unseen is more real than the seen. I can't help but wonder—as we master sensing beyond our five senses, what more might we see? All is not quite how it appears.

The World

Nature is not all bliss. A raging river, a sudden avalanche, or a wild animal can take you away in a second. The world is undergoing significant upheaval and disruption. Mother Earth, as a living organism, mirrors this unrest through her eruptions as she heals, striving to restore harmony and balance.

There is pain to witness and heal, not to ignore or fight against. I never asked to learn about Ascension. In fact, I had a judgment toward those who were taking part in Ascension work, like lightworkers. To me, they were ungrounded, disconnected from their bodies, and didn't want to be on this planet. Being in their bodies was too painful, and the way I saw it, they spent most of their time and energy outside of themselves. My judgment was a mirror for me. I judged others for being "out" of their bodies until the mirror showed me my reflection. That was me—beneath the judgment was my feeling that it is unsafe to be here. I no longer choose to carry the weight of the world on my shoulders.

Like our bodies, the universe is always striving to create the best version of itself. The changes unfolding in every moment are staggering, and its vastness is beyond our human understanding. Even though we can't comprehend it with our minds, we feel it in our hearts.

Change and transformation are constant in life. Nothing stays the same. We are not meant to stay the same. We are meant to evolve. As we embody more light and a higher frequency, a new species of humans is forming, moving the evolution of our biology. Transformation is a constant dynamic process. One that requires commitment, perseverance, and courage. It is not a path for the faint of heart. It is the path of a powerful heart of unconditional love who aligns with and receives support and guidance from the earth and stars.

Multidimensional Body

Once my soul integrated more deeply into my body, I became aware of energy fields extending from me, connecting me to everything around me. My sense expanded outward through my subtle bodies, helping me perceive the energy of others, the collective field, and the channel of Source. As a multidimensional self, I navigate through spaces, sensing beyond my skin. I enter a field of connection where the space within me merges with the space outside, creating a unified energy. The boundaries of my being dissolve into the experience of Oneness. The energy field we all share is boundless in its possibilities, responding to our individual and collective energies.

Conscious Evolution

We are made of energy—we are literally beings of light and vibration. Everything is vibrating. We only see .03 percent of the light spectrum, so we don't see 99.97 percent of reality.

What is reality? Reality emerges from what we allow to exist. Shifting perception changes reality. Bruce Lipton talks about the interplay between our beliefs and perception and how by rewriting our perceptions we rewrite our genes. Exploring this possibility excites me. There is so much that we are beginning to understand...or truly remember.

The more wisdom I integrate, the more questions arise in me. How was that possible? How far can we go? The possibilities are endless in this realm, with our spirit guides cheering us on. Our task is to continue to let the old die and be reborn and open ourselves to the next level of consciousness, which is infinite. Let's keep expanding into the light as the Buddhist rainbow path shows us, for the truth is we are light.

I love being the vessel through which Source flows and creates. As I look back on what I wrote and believed yesterday, I have already changed and expanded.

Looking back over the past few years, I realize that traveling to Ecuador was never part of my life's vision, nor was visiting England on my bucket list. Yet, I was led to explore both places and return again and again. Now my soul families from both countries are connecting in my life. We found each other.

I may have reached this state of unconditional self-love and divine empowerment through my somatic practices, such as mindfulness and breathwork. However, by integrating the wisdom of spirits, sacred plants, animals, and the teachings of indigenous cultures, along with guidance from ascension mentors, archangels, divine masters, and galactic beings, I have truly embodied my soul. I recognize myself as a multidimensional fractal of Source, here to serve.

The outcome of this journey is a deeper recognition of the guidance available to me—the transformative power of integrating through writing. This book began as another way to receive approval from the world. Sharing all of this with you, I have nothing left to hide. I realize I am perfectly imperfect and I am not meant to do this alone.

But when I truly loved myself and everyone unconditionally, that is when my life changed, and it did so very quickly. When my inner world—my thoughts, emotions, energy, and intention—became aligned with the Divine, my life flowed with ease and grace.

As I finish this book, reflecting on my life's journey fills me with immense gratitude for the synchronicities that have now become clear to me. I haven't planned my life. I've followed the threads. Following the threads of guidance has taken me on an incredible journey. Each one is a sign of Source guiding me toward my soul's mission. Woven into an intricate tapestry of places, connections with beings both seen and unseen, and enchanting experiences, they leave me in awe of how they came to be. That is why the indigenous refer to the sacred, divine, Great Spirit, and Source as the Great Mystery.

My goal is not to master everything in life, but rather master the magic configuration I was born with, my Divine blueprint, my design, my chart. As I weave the threads of my divine blueprint into balance, harmony, and order, I align with Divine Will. Each one is a sign of Source guiding me toward my soul's mission—I continue to remember why I came here.

My soul's mission is coming to fruition in this phase of my life. However, this time is different. With self-care, rest, and attunement to guidance, I move forward differently. I no longer need to strive to be of service; I simply am serving by Being. Nurturing a more vibrant world while supporting healing and radiating compassion for those who suffer is a profound revolution of love and remembrance, as I embody the ideals of my childhood heroes, Jesus and Martin Luther King Jr.

While driving Mom to a doctor's appointment the other day, she turned to me and stared. Then she said, "You are a man—you are no longer my baby boy." Forgiveness was the key to reclaiming the Divine Masculine energy—like diving into the darkness was essential to receiving the light. These pathways didn't make sense until I experienced my journey fully. By embracing all of me, every challenge and expansive moment, I became whole. I bow to who I once was.

Mom instilled in me the importance of leaving every place we visited better than we found it. I have embraced this lesson as a guiding principle in my life on this beautiful planet. It reflects the legacy I wish to co-create—to build on what my parents and grandparents were able to accomplish and take it to the next level. To radiate what they were not able to. To honor what they instilled in me and heal what they weren't able to, no longer through judgment but with gratitude and compassion.

The circle of life, from the magic of birth to the mystery of death is a continuous and interconnected journey. This natural balance is intricately interwoven with moments of our earthly existence, all while maintaining a connection to the stars. Shamans live their lives preparing for their death.

The shamans of the Amazon teach of the Jaguar Body—a radiant energy that allows one to dance between worlds. We are beings of light, and in embodying the jaguar, the intention is to leave this life—and this body—in joy, with both ease and power.

I share this intention, and the Divine wills it so.

Much love and many blessings,

Gregg Westwood

"Strength comes from within...
Deep roots are not reached by the frost."
—JRR Tolkien

Reading List

- Almaas, A. H. *Essence: The Diamond Approach to Inner Realization.* Red Wheel Weiser, 1986

- Almaas, A. H. *Facets of Unity: The Enneagram of Holy Ideas.* Shambhala Publications, 2000.

- Almaas, A. H. *Spacecruiser Inquiry: True Guidance for the Inner Journey.* Shambhala Publications, 2002.

- Aposhyan, Susan M. *Body-Mind Psychotherapy: Principles, Techniques, and Practical Applications.* New York: W. W. Norton, 2004.

- Aposhyan, Susan M. *Heart Open, Body Awake: Four Steps to Embodied Spirituality.* Boston: Shambhala Publications, 2021.

- Bass, Ellen, and Laura Davis. *The Courage to Heal: A Guide for Women Survivors of Child Sexual Abuse.* New York: Harper & Row, 1988.

- Brown, Byron. *Soul Without Shame: A Guide to Liberating Yourself from the Judge Within.* Boston: Shambhala Publications, 1999.

- Caldwell, Christine. *Getting Our Bodies Back: Recovery, Healing, and Transformation Through Body-Centered Psychotherapy.* Boston: Shambhala, 1996.

- Cohen, Bonnie Bainbridge. *Sensing, Feeling, and Action: The Experiential Anatomy of Body-Mind Centering®.* 3rd ed. Northampton, MA: Contact Editions, 1993.

- Gendlin, Eugene T. *Focusing*. New York: Bantam Books, 1981.

- Hendricks, Gay. *Learning to Love Yourself: A Guide to Becoming Centered*. New York: Prentice Hall Press, 1982.

- Hendricks, Gay, and Kathlyn Hendricks. *Conscious Loving: The Journey to Co-Commitment*. New York: Bantam Books, 1990.

- Hendricks, Gay. *Conscious Breathing: Breathwork for Health, Stress Release, and Personal Mastery*. New York: Bantam Books, 1995.

- Hendricks, Gay, and Kathlyn Hendricks. *Radiance!: Breathwork, Movement and Body-Centered Psychotherapy*. Berkeley, CA: Wingbow Press, 1991.

- Henricks, Gay. *The Big Leap: Conquer Your Hidden Fear and Take Life to the Next Level*. New York: HarperOne, 2009.

- Lang, Monique. *Meditations and Ceremonies for Healing: A Handbook for Personal Growth and Wellness*. Bloomington, IN: Balboa Press, 2018

- Mission, Sourceness, Sahar Schwaninger, and Dr. Lorna Collins. *Parenting: Book One in Sourceness: A Series for Golden Earth Being*. Book Publishing Plus, December 6, 2024.

- Pennington Wasio, Andrea (1Drea), Gregg Westwood, and Irina Vlada, eds. *Sacred Medicine: Exploring the Psychedelic Hero's Journey: A Transformative Path of Self-Discovery and Spiritual Awakening through Sacred Medicine Ceremonies and Shamanic Rituals*. Make Your Mark Global, 2023.

- Stone, Joshua David. *The Complete Ascension Manual: How to Achieve Ascension in This Lifetime*. Vol. 1 of the *Easy-To-Read Encyclopedia of the Spiritual Path*. Light Technology Publishing, 1994.

Dad's Self Portrait

ACKNOWLEDGMENTS

I am grateful to my father and mother, my ancestors, my brother and sister, and my nieces and nephews. Their love and support have carried me through my years on this planet.

I am blessed to have an abundance of love and support.

To DaeEss 1Drea Pennington Wasio for supporting me and this book from its inception.

To Harry, Greta and Oscar for teaching me and sharing their entire lives with me.

To the Kimberlies in my life—Miss Wonderful, Mrs. Coonce, and Ms. Gladsyz.

To all of my teachers: Michael, Harriet, Maggie, and Marie; Gay and Katie; Calvin; Christine, Nicol and Susan; Jim; Christian and Marjorie, Corrina; Monique and Tati; and Connie.

To Bruce, Chela, Amy, Michelle, Nyra and Susanne.

To Paula, Brian and Tama.

To KC, Eli, Tom, and Daniel.

To Sharon, Nancy, Hilda, Annette and Lea

To Barry and Lorna.

To my editors, Micheal and Zora.

To my publishers, Kristen and Maira.

To the indigenous people of North and South America and England.

To the directions, the elements, the spirits, and this sacred earth—her animals and plants, especially Grandmother, the trees and birds.

And to the Source of all creation.

"May you be at peace. May your heart remain open.
May you awaken to the light of your own true nature.
May you be healed. May you be a source of healing for all beings."
—Tibetan prayer

Thank You for Reading *Rooted Soul*

May this journey to the depths of your soul be your companion as you continue to remember the wholeness that was never truly lost. If you feel called to deepen your path to authentic expression and multidimensional embodiment, I invite you to explore more resources and connect with our community: www.depthintegration.com.

Discover transformative practices, sacred wisdom teachings, and opportunities to join our global community of souls committed to conscious embodiment. Whether through events, workshops, immersive retreats, or the *Our Souls Speak* podcast, there are many pathways to support your ongoing realization of Oneness.

Your embodied awakening is not just a personal healing—it's an offering to the collective consciousness of humanity. As you continue to inhabit your sacred vessel with presence and reverence, you contribute to the fullest realization of what is possible now.

The path to wholeness is eternal, and I am honored to walk alongside you as you remember the multidimensional being you've always been.

In service to your authentic embodiment and our collective awakening,

Gregg Westwood
Instagram / LinkedIn / YouTube

ABOUT THE AUTHOR

Gregg Westwood is a former actor, dancer, massage therapist, and spiritual seeker who has dedicated his life to healing, embodiment, authentic self-expression, and service. With over 35 years of experience in somatic psychology, he integrates creative arts, indigenous wisdom traditions, and multidimensional awareness into his work, which he terms Depth Integration. Gregg mentors clients, facilitates retreats and workshops internationally, and creates transformative spaces for embodied soul integration.

His journey in counseling began in 1985 as part of GMHC's Buddy Program in New York City, where he supported caregivers during the early AIDS crisis. He holds a Master's degree in Somatic Psychology and has taught at Heartwood Institute and Naropa University. Additionally, his credentials include certifications in massage therapy, hypnotherapy, Polarity Therapy, and Transformational Therapy (based on the Hendricks Method), along with training in Pilates and Educational Kinesiology and studies in ParaYoga, the Diamond Heart Approach, and the Integrated Beingness Programme.

Gregg is the co-host of the *Our Souls Speak* podcast and the host of the Healing Trauma through Conscious Embodiment and Conscious Embodiment summits. He is also a featured author in *Sacred Medicine* and *Dare to Dream*.